A THEOLOGY OF TESTAMENT
IN THE YOUNG LUTHER
THE LECTURES ON HEBREWS

STUDIES
IN MEDIEVAL AND
REFORMATION THOUGHT

EDITED BY

HEIKO A. OBERMAN, Tübingen

IN COOPERATION WITH
E. JANE DEMPSEY DOUGLASS, Claremont, California
LEIF GRANE, Copenhagen
GUILLAUME H. M. POSTHUMUS MEYJES, Leiden
ANTON G. WEILER, Nijmegen

VOLUME XII

KENNETH HAGEN

A THEOLOGY OF TESTAMENT
IN THE YOUNG LUTHER
THE LECTURES ON HEBREWS

LEIDEN
E. J. BRILL
1974

A THEOLOGY OF TESTAMENT
IN THE YOUNG LUTHER
THE LECTURES ON HEBREWS

BY

KENNETH HAGEN

LEIDEN
E. J. BRILL
1974

ISBN   90 04 03987 2

PRINTED IN BELGIUM

TABLE OF CONTENTS

PREFACE

My interest in the "young Luther" and his *Lectures on Hebrews* during the critical years, 1517-18, began in 1962 at Harvard and resulted in a dissertation and several articles. For extensive guidance during that period I owe a great deal to my major advisor, Professor Heiko A. Oberman. I also received much from Professors Krister Stendahl and George H. Williams, as well as from the librarians Dr. James Tanis and Dr. Maria Grossmann. All were at Harvard at the time.

My interest in the "young Luther" and "the Hebrews" has continued and this study was stimulated by my concern to deal with some recent work on the young Luther (cf. the Introduction), and by the research of the many students in my Luther seminars at Marquette. Several research grants from Marquette have made publication of the study possible. For his editorial assistance I wish to thank especially my colleague at Marquette, Thomas Caldwell, S.J. Also of assistance were Nicholas Balducci and Emily Pfizenmaier. Earlier preparation of the manuscript was made possible by Lorna Rixman. Any non-docetic scholar survives only in a thoroughly human context and that context has been provided me by my wife and children.

May 29, 1974   Kenneth HAGEN

LIST OF ABBREVIATIONS

CCSL *Corpus Christianorum, Series Latina* Turnholti, 1953 ff.

CSEL *Corpus Scriptorum Ecclesiasticorum Latinorum* Vienna, 1866 ff.

HR Emanuel Hirsch and Hans Rückert, *Luthers Vorlesung über den Hebräerbrief nach der Vatikanischen Handschrift* "Arbeiten zur Kirchengeschichte," Vol. 13, Berlin, 1929.

LW American Edition of *Luther's Works*, Jaroslav Pelikan and Helmut T. Lehmann, gen. eds. Philadelphia and St. Louis, 1955 ff.

PG *Patrologia, Series Graeca* 161 Vols., Ed. J. P. Migne, Paris, 1857-1866.

PL *Patrologia, Series Latina* 221 Vols. in 222, Ed. J. P. Migne, Paris, 1844-1904.

WA *D. Martin Luthers Werke Kritische Gesamtausgabe* Weimar, 1883 ff.

WA Br *D. Martin Luthers Werke: Briefwechsel* Weimar, 1930-1948.

WA DB *D. Martin Luthers Werke: Deutsche Bibel* Weimar, 1906-1961.

WA Tr *D. Martin Luthers Werke: Tischreden* Weimar, 1912-1921.

INTRODUCTION

Several advances have been made in our understanding of the young Luther since the beginning of the "Luther Renaissance." The Lortz school reads the young Luther in the light of medieval spirituality.[1] The post-Lortz, Catholic scholars no longer blame the "tragedy" of the Reformation on the later Middle Ages.[2] The great students of Karl Holl read Luther as a creative theologian in the tradition of *Dogmengeschichte*.[3] Oberman relates the young Luther to Nominalism and Mysticism.[4] Ebeling initiated interest in relating Luther to medieval hermeneutics.[5] This was further advanced with the beginning made on Luther's first exegetical work, *Lectures on the Psalms* (1513-16).[6] As a part of that effort to study the development of the Christian Church in terms of the history of biblical exegesis, this study began as an examination of Luther's *Lectures on Hebrews* (1517-18).[7]

Interest in Luther's early exegesis has been confined largely to the *Lectures on the Psalms* and the *Lectures on Romans* (1515-16). Examination of the *Lectures on Hebrews* revealed that a most fruitful way of understanding the main thrust of the exegesis was to look over Luther's shoulder at the exegetical sources on his desk, in his head, "in the air." The study quickly became an analysis of the development of "Western" commentaries on Hebrews, beginning with Chrysostom, in Latin translation, the most influential work on Hebrews in the Middle Ages. Other major turning points in the medieval exegesis of Hebrews occurred with the *Glossa*, St. Thomas, whose influence can be seen on the great Nicholas of Lyra, Faber and Erasmus, whose textual analyses aided early Reformation exegesis. Augustine, although he did not write a commentary on Hebrews, has been included.

---

[1] Joseph Lortz, *Die Reformation in Deutschland* (4th ed.; Freiburg, 1962).

[2] Otto H. Pesch, O.P., *Theologie der Rechtfertigung bei Martin Luther und Thomas von Aquin: Versuch eines systematisch-theologischen Dialogs* (Mainz, 1967).

[3] Karl Holl, *Gesammelte Aufsätze zur Kirchengeschichte* Vol. I: *Luther* (6th ed.; Tübingen, 1932).

[4] Heiko Oberman, " 'Facientibus quod in se est Deus non denegat gratiam' Robert Holcot, O.P. and the Beginnings of Luther's Theology," *Harvard Theological Review* 55 (1962), pp. 317-42.

[5] Gerhard Ebeling, *Evangelische Evangelienauslegung* (Munich, 1942).

[6] Martin Luther, *Dictata super Psalterium*, in *WA* 55.I and II (Weimar, 1939).

[7] Martin Luther, *Divi Pauli apostoli ad Hebreos epistola*, in *WA* 57.III (Weimar, 1939).

In its approach, this work marks a departure from the other studies of Luther's *Lectures on Hebrews* (detailed in Chapter One), including the recent study of J. P. Boendermaker.[8] Although Boendermaker does compare Luther to medieval exegesis, 1) the base of his comparison is incomplete, 2) the comparison has no apparent relevant function in his treatment of "Important Theological Concepts found in Luther's Lectures" and 3) his interest in the "young Luther" is largely limited to Luther's reported "conversion" experience and the influence of "the mystical tradition" on him.

The most recent work on the *Lectures on Hebrews*, that of H. Feld,[9] was a final push I needed to publish this study. Feld as well as Boendermaker simply misses the whole point of the *Lectures on Hebrews*. By his heavily exegetical (in the modern sense) comparison of Steinbach and Luther, Feld does not have sufficient perspective to see that Luther is dealing with a very traditional and theological judgment about the main message of Hebrews, a judgment of which Steinbach and/or Feld are apparently not aware. Feld's dichotomy between exegesis and theology is dubious because Luther's exegesis is theological and his theology exegetical, reflecting an effort on his part to join together what Aristotle had put asunder.[10]

Medieval exegesis of Hebrews concerned itself first and foremost with the question of the theological relationship between the two Testaments. Augustine's thought on this subject will be consulted. This will help nuance the possibilities and broaden the base for relating Luther to his predecessors. The category of *testamentum* will be primary for developing this relationship. The examination of Augustine will show that in dealing with the relationship between the two Testaments one must differentiate hermeneutical concerns with the two books, providential concerns with the two eras, and soteriological concerns with faith.

A significant part of the discussion of the two Testaments for medieval exegetes and for Luther are the themes of faith and Christology. A comparison of Luther and medieval exegesis on these themes

---

[8] J. P. Boendermaker, *Luthers Commentaar op de Brief aan de Hebreeën 1517-1518* (Assen, 1965).

[9] Helmut Feld, *Martin Luthers und Wendelin Steinbachs Vorlesungen über den Hebräerbrief. Eine Studie zur Geschichte der neutestamentlichen Exegese und Theologie* ("Veröffentlichungen des Institutes für europäische Geschichte Mainz," Vol. 62; Wiesbaden, 1971).

[10] Beryl Smalley, *The Study of the Bible in the Middle Ages* (Oxford, 1952), pp. 293-94.

will reveal that aspects of Luther's interpretation come to light through a comparison with medieval exegesis that are not otherwise apparent, since Luther often deals with issues and questions raised by medieval exegetes without saying so. Often the force of Luther's interpretation comes to light only when one realizes that Luther is opposing or qualifying a medieval interpretation.

Additional significance of Luther's interpretation is seen by a comparison of his earlier exegesis of Hebrews texts and Psalm texts used in Hebrews with his *Lectures on Hebrews*. By this comparison some attention is given to other works of the young Luther.

This study will proceed, then, by locating Luther's text, giving some account of its interpretation, and discover what importance Luther attached to Hebrews (Chapter One). Chapter Two will develop medieval discussions of the relationship between the two Testaments and compare Luther to these discussions. St. Augustine's theology will be important for this problem. Chapters Three and Four will round out this important theological problem for the young Luther by relating Luther's concept of faith and Christology to the medieval exegetical tradition.

An editorial note regarding capitalization of Old Testament/New Testament: when referring to book and/or era, thus hermeneutical and/or providential categories, upper case will be used. When testament (o.t./n.t.) is a soteriological category, lower case will be used.

CHAPTER ONE

LUTHER'S LECTURES ON HEBREWS

A. Text

Every Monday and Friday from 12:00-1:00 p.m. at the University in Wittenberg during the summer and winter semesters of 1517-18[1] (April 21, 1517, to March 26, 1518)[2] the majority of theological students gathered to hear Martin Luther lecture on the Epistle to the Hebrews. Luther had been lecturing on the Bible since the summer semester of 1513 and had become increasingly popular with the students. Many men were coming to Wittenberg for the express purpose of hearing Luther. Townspeople were also attracted to this young professor of the Bible. John Oldecop reports that Luther was exciting because he sometimes used "such stout German."[3]

John Lang wrote to George Spalatin on March 10, 1516, that the lectures on the Bible in Wittenberg were being well received by many students. This letter shows that Luther was attracting the majority of theological students and that the lectures on the scholastics were very poorly attended:

> Very many students are all excited and enthusiastic about the lectures on the Bible and the early Fathers, whereas the study of the scholastic doctors (as they are called) attract maybe two or three students.[4]

This trend continued, as we can see from Luther's letter to Lang on May 18, 1517, shortly after he had begun his lectures on Hebrews:

> Our theology and St. Augustine are progressing well, and with God's help rule

---

[1] *WA* 57.III.xix.

[2] HR xxvi-xxvii. Oswald Bayer has recently challenged this standard dating (*Promissio: Geschichte der reformatorischen Wende in Luthers Theologie* ["Forschungen zur Kirchen- und Dogmengeschichte," Vol. 24; Göttingen, 1971], pp. 203-206.) On the basis of coordinating similar specific themes in the *Lectures on Hebrews* and other writings of 1517-18, he suggests rather the winter and summer semesters of 1517-18 (Oct. 1517 to Sept. 1518).

[3] Heinrich Böhmer, *Der junge Luther*, ed. Heinrich Bornkamm (Stuttgart, 1951), pp. 133-34.

[4] Kenneth Hagen, "An Addition to the Letters of John Lang: Introduction and Translation," *Archiv für Reformationsgeschichte* 60 (1969), p. 31.

at our University.... Indeed no one can expect to have any students if he does
not want to teach this theology, that is, lecture on the Bible or on St. Augustine
or another [authoritative doctor in the Church].[5]

Luther lectured on Hebrews, as he had done on the Psalms, Romans
and Galatians, in the traditional manner by dividing his material
into Gloss and Scholium. It was the last time that he proceeded in
this manner. For his preparations Luther glossed his special copy of
the Latin Vulgate by inserting short summary and descriptive phrases
between the lines of the text (traditionally known throughout the
Middle Ages as the interlinear gloss) and by adding more extended
exegetical material in the margins (traditionally known as the marginal
or ordinary gloss). Luther also worked out his own extensive exegetical
and theological interpretation of Hebrews (traditionally known as
scholium).

Luther's lectures consisted of dictating his own Gloss and then
his Scholium. Each student had his own copy of the Vulgate, which
Luther had had printed especially for his class. The student then
glossed his own text with the interlinear and marginal Glosses as
well as with the Scholium that Luther dictated. Student lecture notes
were all that survived of Luther's lectures on Hebrews. Luther's
own lecture notes are not extant.

Only two sets of student lecture notes have survived. One of these
was the notes of chapters 1-5 of the Scholium taken by Sigismund
Reichenbach,[6] and in the mid-sixteenth century another set of student
lecture notes was copied by Aurifaber and someone else (designated
as m[II]).[7] Then for well over 300 years these two sets of student notes
lay dormant, unknown to the world of Luther scholarship.

It has been only recently that Luther's lectures on Hebrews have
been edited and published. In 1899 Hermann Vopel and Johannes
Ficker discovered Aurifaber's copy of student notes in the Vatican
Library (abbreviated "P").[8] Ficker also made another important
discovery in 1904: Reichenbach's lecture notes, the so-called Dessau
manuscript (abbreviated "D").

"D" is important not only because it provides a check on "P" but
also because it is an earlier witness to Luther's lectures. Ficker, how-

---

[5] *LW* 48. 42; *WA Br* 1. 99. 8ff.

[6] *WA* 57. III. xi.

[7] *WA* 57. III. vii.

[8] The manuscript Pal. lat. 1825 contained *Divi Pauli apostoli ad Hebreos* (Gloss)
and *D M L Commentariolus in epistolam divi Pauli apostoli ad Hebreos: 1517* (Scholium).

ever, was reluctant to publish an edition of the lectures, partly because he never gave up the hope that additional material might be discovered. Finally in 1929, tired of waiting for Ficker's edition,[9] Emanuel Hirsch and Hanns Rückert came out with a critical edition of the Vatican manuscript.[10]

Shortly after the appearance of the Hirsch-Rückert edition, Ficker published his critical edition.[11] In addition to "P" and "D", Ficker also used Rörer's notes of Nikolaus von Amsdorf's lectures on Hebrews (abbreviated "A"), delivered in Wittenberg during the summer of 1521.[12] The importance of Amsdorf's lectures is that in them he frequently quotes from Luther's lectures on Hebrews.[13]

Ficker also prepared the Weimar edition of Luther's lectures on *Divi Pauli Apostoli ad Hebreos Epistola* (*WA* 57, Weimar, 1939). For the Weimar edition, Ficker reworked his previous edition by giving more authority to "D" and by providing a more complete apparatus.[14]

The English translation of Luther's *Lectures on Hebrews* by James Atkinson in the *Library of Christian Classics*[15] I have shown elsewhere

---

[9] Otto Scheel, "Die Textausgaben der Vorlesung Luthers über den Hebräerbrief," *Theologische Studien und Kritiken* 102 (1930), pp. 202-04.

[10] *Luthers Vorlesung über den Hebräerbrief nach der Vatikanischen Handschrift* ("Arbeiten zur Kirchengeschichte," Vol. 13; Berlin, 1929): "Das Hauptbedenken, das gegen unsre Ausgabe erhoben werden könnte, ist, dass wir allein die vatikanische Handschrift, nicht auch die Dessauer zugrunde legen konnten. Aber die Dessauer Handschrift ist für die Allgemeinheit unzugänglich, und nach dem Wenigen, das über sie bekannt ist, haben wir eine wesentliche Erschütterung unsrer Ausgabe wohl nicht zu befürchten" (p. v).

[11] *Luthers Vorlesung über den Hebräerbrief 1517-18* ("Anfänge reformatorischer Bibelauslegung," Vol. 2; Leipzig, 1929).

[12] "Auf A (Zwickauer Ratschulbibliothek, Rohtsches Ms. XXXVII), eine Nachschrift Rörers von der bis Kap. 15, 15 reichenden Vorlesung, die Amsdorf im Sommer 1521 in Wittenberg über den Hebräerbrief gehalten hat, ist damit schon im Vorausgehenden hingewiesen: eine nur mittelbare, aber doch für die Sicherung von Textstellen (auch einer grösseren, des ersten Teils der Scholie zu Kap. 5, 1) der Vorlesung Luthers wertvolle Quelle" (*WA* 57. III. xv).

[13] Ficker, *Anfänge ref. Bibelauslegung* 2, p. xxii.

[14] *WA* 57. III. xxvii.

[15] *Luther: Early Theological Works,* ("Library of Christian Classics," Vol. 16). *Luther's Lectures on Hebrews,* ed. Pelikan ("Luther's Work," Vol. 29; St. Louis, 1968), pp.109-241, has subsequently appeared. The translations in this work are the author's, which are appended to his Harvard dissertation, 1966.

to be replete with inconsistencies, errors of omission and addition, as well as other mistakes of both minor and major consequence.[16]

B. INTERPRETATION

A few years after the appearance of the two independent critical editions in 1929[17] several articles, one monograph, and two books appeared.[18] Luther's lectures have been examined in secondary literature from the perspective of their relation either to the thought of Erasmus (Vogelsang), the thought of Augustine (Hamel), the so-called *Turmerlebnis* problem (especially, Gyllenkrok and Bizer), the contemporary effort by New Testament scholars to interpret Hebrews (Baruzi), selected writings of Luther (Thimme), the development of Luther's *theologia crucis* (Ellwein), Luther's exegesis of 10,5 (Brandenburg), "the exegetical tradition" and "mystical theology" (Boendermaker), or to Steinbach's commentary on Hebrews (Feld).

Erich Vogelsang, the author of the monograph, made a study of the newly published *Lectures on Hebrews* from the perspective of Luther's relation to Humanism.[19] Feld's perspective is largely the same. In his *Lectures on Hebrews*, according to Vogelsang, Luther had developed into a first-rate exegete, with all the scientific tools of Humanism at his disposal. In fact, Luther's primary interest in these lectures is philological.[20] Luther's Humanism in these lectures consisted of the fact that exegesis as science had priority for him. Secondly, he had extensive interest in the basic Greek and Hebrew texts and languages. And thirdly, he appropriated the Humanists'

---

[16] "The First Translation of Luther's *Lectures on Hebrews*: A Review Article," *Church History* 34 (1965), pp. 204-13.

[17] Two German translations appeared in 1930. Erich Vogelsang did a translation based on the Hirsch-Rückert text (*Luthers Hebräerbriefvorlesung 1517-18: Deutsche Übersetzung* ["Arbeiten zur Kirchengeschichte," Vol. 17; Berlin, 1930]), and Georg Helbig based his translation on Ficker's text (*Martin Luther Vorlesung über den Hebräerbrief 1517-18* [Leipzig, 1930]). Cf. Peter Barth, "Luther zum Hebräerbrief," *Die Christliche Welt* 44 (1930) p. 957, and Edward Ellwein, "Zu Luthers Hebräerbriefvorlesung," *Zwischen den Zeiten* 9 (1931), p. 549.

[18] The articles of Scheel, Barth and Ellwein have been referred to in the footnotes above since they deal mainly with the text and editions of these lectures.

[19] Erich Vogelsang, *Die Bedeutung der neuveroffentlichten Hebräerbriefvorlesung Luthers von 1517-18: Ein Beitrag zur Frage: Humanismus und Reformation* (Tübingen, 1930).

[20] *Ibid.*, p. 7.

critical stance over against the traditional understanding of a given text.[21]

Though Luther learned much from the Humanists, Vogelsang shows that he was critical of them. For example, Luther learned the philological signifiancce of repentance (*poenitentiam agite*)—*resipiscite*—from the Humanists; however he used it against them. For Erasmus *resipiscite* meant a rational, ethical enlightenment. But for Luther it meant the *transitus cordis*, a central theme in the *Lectures on Hebrews*. Thus Luther was in the same position in relation to Erasmus in 1517 as he was in 1525.[22]

The most decisive distinction between Humanism and the Reformation according to Vogelsang is that Luther did not approach Scripture with the purpose of bolstering his own ideas by critical exegesis, as did the Humanists, but rather let himself stand under the criticism of the Word.[23]

Finally, Vogelsang summarizes the Reformation theology contained in Luther's lectures. Faith and Christology for Vogelsang are the two central themes in Luther's *Lectures on Hebrews*.[24] Luther's new and peculiar concept of faith in these lectures is that faith is existential and is concerned with personal certitude.[25] Perhaps the most significant discovery in his *Lectures on Hebrews* is that, like Kierkegaard, Luther discovered the individual.[26]

Luther's Christology, according to Vogelsang, emphasizes that Christ identified himself with lost humanity and made it possible for us to identify ourselves with him. Atonement has two sides: what Christ did for us and what he does in us. Christ experienced and overcame the cross, temptation, death and judgment so that we, like him, might conquer the cross, temptation, death and judgment.[27] The work of Christ involves his exinanition (Heb. 2), his high priestly character (Heb. 5) and his testament (Heb. 9). Luther's concept of the exinanition of Christ is evident for the first time in his *Lectures on Hebrews*. The emphasis is not on the divinity but on the humanity

---

[21] *Ibid.*, pp. 8-10.
[22] *Ibid.*, pp. 11-12.
[23] *Ibid.*, p. 13.
[24] *Ibid.*, pp. 15-21.
[25] *Ibid.*, pp. 16-17.
[26] *Ibid.*, p. 17.
[27] *Ibid.*, p. 19.

of Christ and, therefore, not on the incarnation but on the cross and death. Regarding the believer, the emphasis is on *Anfechtung*.[28]

For the first time in Luther's writings, Vogelsang argues, we see a developed doctrine of the Eucharist, developed before his controversy with the reformed theologians. The Lord's Supper is a testament of the dying Christ, which contains the promise of forgiveness and which is received by faith.[29]

Jean Baruzi examined Luther's *Lectures on Hebrews* more from a New Testament point of view.[30] He used Luther's lectures as an aid to the contemporary problem of understanding the Epistle to the Hebrews.[31] Baruzi considers his general interest in the young Luther to be on the subject of Paul and Luther.[32]

Baruzi, acknowledging the "très fine étude" of Vogelsang, holds that the philological and "scientific" interest of Luther is striking.[33] Baruzi summarizes in short order the theological interest of Luther. The main themes are faith and Christology.[34]

Alfred Jørgensen made a general survey of Luther's *Lectures on Hebrews*.[35] Of greatest interest for Jørgensen is the theology contained in the lectures.[36] Jørgensen summarizes the theological content of the lectures under the following headings: knowledge of God, law, gospel, Christology, anthropology, justification, sacraments, predestination, penance and Church.

Hans Thimme studied Luther's Christology in Luther's *Lectures on Hebrews*. He did so from the perspective of four documents, covering the early and later Luther.[37] The significance of Christ in the commentary on Hebrews is that "Christus=iustitia dei=fides."[38]

---

[28] *Ibid.*, pp. 19-21.

[29] *Ibid.*, pp. 20-21.

[30] Jean Baruzi, "Le commentaire de Luther à l'Épître aux Hébreux," *Revue d'Histoire et de Philosophie Religieuses* 11 (1931), pp. 461-98.

[31] *Ibid.*, pp. 470-80.

[32] *Ibid.*, p. 498.

[33] *Ibid.*, p. 467.

[34] *Ibid.*, pp. 486-95.

[35] Alfred Jørgensen, "Luthers forelaesning over Hebraeerbrevet," *For laere og liv. Festskrift til Det teologiske Menighetsfakultets 25års jubilaeum* (Oslo, 1933), pp. 176-204.

[36] *Ibid.*, p. 185.

[37] Hans Thimme, *Christi Bedeutung für Luthers Glauben. Unter Zugrundelegung des Romerbrief—des Hebräerbrief—des Galaterbriefkommentars von 1531, und der Disputationem* (Gütersloh, 1933).

[38] *Ibid.*, pp. 46, 49.

Adolf Hamel has studied Luther's *Lectures on Hebrews* from the perspective of Luther's relation to Augustine.[39] He agrees with the work of Vogelsang and Thimme. Hamel goes beyond Vogelsang's discussion of Luther's concept of faith. He agrees with Vogelsang that for the first time in Luther's writings we have his fully-developed concept of faith as constituting man's relationship to God. But then Hamel says more, namely, that Luther's concept of faith is bound to his theology of the Word. Faith is hearing the Word and *adhaesio verbo Dei* (Ps. 73,28). This text is a favorite of both Luther's and Augustine's; however they differ fundamentally in their interpretation of it. For Augustine, man's adherence to God is consummated in a substantial immediacy with God, his *summum bonum* and final rest, through the Spirit and love; whereas for Luther a distance between God and man is maintained. For God acts through his Word and man responds by hearing.[40]

Eduard Ellwein examined these lectures of Luther's from the perspective of the development of Luther's *theologia crucis*.[41] Ellwein spends most of his time summarizing and quoting Luther's statements about "solus Christus" and "sola fides." However, the unifying theme and red-thread throughout the commentary is Luther's *theologia crucis*. All lines come together in Luther's Gloss on Heb. 12,11.[42]

In more contemporary studies Luther's *Lectures on Hebrews* have been studied in the light of the so-called *Turmerlebnis* problem. The two best known are the books by Axel Gyllenkrok[43] and Ernst Bizer.[44] They claim that these lectures are of revolutionary importance because in them Luther has come to see that the Word—the promise, or the Gospel—is the means of grace. In short, Luther has discovered the "Reformation" meaning of *iustitia dei passiva*.

The key to Luther's discovery for Gyllenkrok is *Heilsgewissheit*.[45]

---

[39] Adolf Hamel, *Der junge Luther und Augustin, ihre Beziehungen in der Recht-fertigungslehre nach Luthers ersten vorlesungen 1509-18* Vol. 2 (Gütersloh, 1935).

[40] *Ibid.*, pp. 149-51.

[41] Edward Ellwein, "Die Entfaltung der theologia crucis in Luthers Hebräerbrief-vorlesung," *Theologische Aufsätze: Karl Barth zum 50. Geburtstag* (Munich, 1936), pp. 382-404.

[42] *Ibid.*, p. 401.

[43] Axel Gyllenkrok, *Rechtfertigung und Heiligung in der frühen evangelischen Theologie Luthers* (Uppsala, 1952).

[44] Ernst Bizer, *Fides ex auditu. Eine Untersuchung über die Entdeckung der Gerechtig-keit Gottes durch Martin Luther* (3rd ed.; Darmstadt, 1966).

[45] Gyllenkrok, p. 72.

Gyllenkrok's argument is that in the lectures on Psalms and Romans, Luther is working with a *humilitas*-theology which is Augustinian.[46] In the Scholium on Rom. 8,16 a beginning of a break between his *humilitas*-theology and an evangelical theology is evident.[47] Luther finally works out the problem of *Heilsgewissheit* in his *Lectures on Hebrews* and in a sermon preached during the Leipzig disputation. The solution to the problem is that faith comes from hearing the Word.[48]

The key to Luther's *Turmerlebnis* according to Bizer is a theology of the Word that teaches that the Word itself is the means of grace.[49] Faith justifies as direct response to the Word and as a substitute for humility.[50] The Word is not a moral, legal encouragement to appropriate Christ's humility, but is the means of grace whereby man is justified.[51] Faith which comes from hearing the Word brings certitude of salvation.[52] The sacraments are effectual means of grace to the believer because they are bound up with the Word.[53]

With regard to the development of the "young Luther" Bizer argues that in his lectures on Psalms and Romans, Luther is immersed in the *humilitas*-theology of the Middle Ages whereby faith is the basis for humility which one attains by tropologically appropriating the work of Christ-humility.[54] Humility justifies. However, in his Scholia on Heb. 5,1, 7,1, 7,12, 9,17 and 9,24, Luther is beginning to come to a new understanding of law and Gospel, faith, certitude of salvation and the sacraments.[55] In general the *Lectures on Hebrews* are transitional.[56] In the *Acta Augustana* and parallel literature of 1518-19, there are mature, self-conscious and clear theological state-

---

[46] *Ibid.*, p. 4.

[47] *Ibid.*, p. 67.

[48] *Ibid.*, pp. 72-74. Cf. also p. 75: "Die höchstmögliche Gewissheit dürfte erreicht sein, wenn Luther nicht nur meint, dass das Wort das Heil enthält und schenkt, sondern wenn es selbst das Heil auch gleichzeitig verheisst, wenn also *die promissio mit dem heilsbringenden Evangelium identisch wird.*"

[49] Bizer, p. 7.

[50] *Ibid.*, pp. 77, 80-81.

[51] *Ibid.*, pp. 164, 167.

[52] *Ibid.*, p. 91.

[53] *Ibid.*, pp. 92, 103.

[54] *Ibid.*, pp. 22, 51.

[55] *Ibid.*, pp. 80-92.

[56] *Ibid.*, p. 75.

ments about the understanding and implications of *fides ex auditu*.[57] The date of Luther's *Turmerlebnis*, therefore, according to Bizer is the spring or summer of 1518.[58]

"Ears are the only organs of the Christian man" is an example for Albert Brandenburg that all of Luther's theology is grounded in the Word and in the hearing of the Word.[59]

The recent study of Luther's *Lectures on Hebrews* is the *Academisch Proefschrift* of Boendermaker. Boendermaker has undertaken his study from the perspective of the commentaries on Hebrews by Chrysostom, the *Glossa* and Lyra, whom he designates as "de oude exegese" or "de traditionele exegese."[60] A large portion of Boendermaker's work is a listing, chapter by chapter, of "Important agreements" and "Important disagreements" between Luther and the *Glossa*, Lyra and Chrysostom.

Boendermaker also considers "Some of the Important Theological Concepts in Luther's Commentary and Their Significance for the Development of His Reformation Theology up to 1518." They are: *Conformitas, Transitus, Exemplum* and *Sacramentum*, the Sacraments, Faith and *Theologia crucis*. These important concepts, according to Boendermaker, bear the influence of "mystical theology."[61]

The most recent work on *Lectures on Hebrews* is the revised dissertation of Helmut Feld comparing the Wittenberg lectures with those of Wendelin Steinbach begun in Tübingen a year earlier.[62] The main portion and interest of the study is the philological relationship of Steinbach and Luther to Humanism. Melanchthon's judgment that Steinbach was a humanist and a precursor of the Reformation must be balanced, according to Feld, by Steinbach's dependence on medieval and scholastic thought and the authority of the Church.[63] Feld also treats the standard topics of faith, certitude, justification, Christology, and Word.

---

[57] *Ibid.*, pp. 115 ff.

[58] *Ibid.*, p. 7.

[59] Albert Brandenburg, "*Solae aures sunt organa Christiani hominis.* Zu Luthers Exegese von Hebr. 10, 5f.," *Einsicht und Glaube. Gottlieb Sohngen zum 70. Geburtstag*, ed. Ratzinger and Fries (Freiburg, 1962), pp. 401-404.

[60] Boendermaker, p. 74.

[61] *Ibid.*, pp. 85, 90, 100, 101, 107, 108, 110 and 114.

[62] Helmut Feld, *Martin Luthers und Wendelin Steinbachs Vorlesungen über den Hebräerbrief*.

[63] *Ibid.*, pp. 19, 212-13.

Each of these secondary sources is valuable from its limited perspective. However, the task remains to examine Luther's exegesis of Hebrews in the light of medieval exegesis.

Boendermaker's study examines Luther's relation to some of the medieval exegetes of Hebrews. However, his work is incomplete. He limits his study to the exegesis of Chrysostom, the *Glossa* and Lyra, but then proceeds to summarize their relation to Luther by describing them as *"the* exegetical tradition." Boendermaker does not even treat all the medieval exegetes whom Luther explicitly quotes in his lectures-Valla, Faber and Erasmus. Besides there are a number of other exegetes of Hebrews who are important representatives of the medieval exegetical tradition, namely, Alcuin, Aquinas, Tarantasia and Dionysius the Carthusian.[64] The inclusion of Augustine revolutionizes the task.

C. MEDIEVAL EXEGESIS

What medieval commentaries on Hebrews then, more adequately constitute Luther's relation to the medieval exegetical tradition?[65]

---

[64] In addition to generalizing about the "exegetical tradition" Boendermaker also frequently and vaguely refers to "mystical theology" without realizing that there are many mystical theologies (e.g., Erich Vogelsang, "Luther und die Mystik," *Luther-Jahrbuch* 19 [Weimar, 1937], pp. 32-54).

[65] Bibliographies of medieval commentaries on Hebrews are scant. In addition to the critical editions of Hirsch-Rückert and Ficker, Denifle's study of Western exegesis of Rom. 1:17 is of some help for locating texts, though not everyone who commented on Romans also commented on Hebrews: Heinrich Denifle, O.P., *Die abendländischen Schriftausleger bis Luther über "Justitia Dei" (Rom. 1:17) und "Justificatio,"* Vol. I, Part 2 (2nd ed., "Luther und Luthertum;" Mainz, 1905). C. Spicq, O.P., in his *L'Épître aux Hébreux* (Paris, 1952), has an annotated "Bibliographie" which is a general survey of the exegesis of Hebrews from the Eastern commentaries of the ancient Church up to our own time. More valuable for its almost exhaustive bibliography is Fridericus Stegmüller's *Repertorium Biblicum Medii Aevi* (7 vols.; Madrid, 1950-61). Stegmüller lists both manuscript and printed copies. Cf. Ulfridus van Camp, O.F.M., "Bibliographia," *De Habitudine Missae ad Sacrificium Crucis apud Commentatores latinos Epistolae ad Hebraeos usque ad Petrum Lombardum* ("Pontificium Athenaeum Antonianum Facultas Theologica. Theses ad Lauream N. 151," Katanga, 1962), pp. vii-xvi. For complete manuscript listings of the medieval Hermits of the Order of St. Augustine see Adolar Zumkeller, "Manuskripte von Werken der Autoren des Augustiner-Eremitenordens in mitteleuropäischen Bibliotheken," *Augustiniana* 11 (1961), pp. 27-86, 261-319, 478-532; 12 (1962), pp. 27-92, 299-357; 13 (1963), pp. 418-73; 14 (1964), pp. 105-62. Eduard Riggenbach has made a study of the early medieval Latin commentaries on

First of all, there are the commentaries which Luther actually used. Then, there are those which are used in the notes of the critical editions. And finally, there are some other commentaries which help to fill out our understanding of medieval exegesis.

The commentaries cited by Luther in his lectures are those of Chrysostom, the *Glossa*, Lyra, Burgos, Doering, Valla, Faber and Erasmus. Later in his life Luther said that St. John Chrysostom's *Homilies on Hebrews*[66] was his main source for the *Lectures on Hebrews*:

> Let them take a book of the Bible and look up the interpretations of the Fathers and the same thing will happen to them that happened to me when I took up the Epistle to the Hebrews with the Gloss of St. Chrysostom, Titus and Galatians with the help of St. Jerome, Genesis with the help of St. Ambrose and St. Augustine, the Psalter with all the exegetes that I could find and so on.[67]

Luther quotes Chrysostom more than any other author. In fact, throughout the Middle Ages Chrysostom's homilies, in Latin translation, exerted a great deal of influence and were read, quoted and interpreted by most exegetes of Hebrews.[68]

Hebrews: *Historische Studien zum Hebräerbrief*. Part I: *Die ältesten lateinischen Kommentare zum Hebräerbrief* ("Forschungen zur Geschichte des neutestamentlichen Kanons und der altkirchlichen Literatur;" Leipzig, 1907). A. Landgraf has worked on the Pauline commentaries of the twelfth century: "Familienbildung bei Paulinenkommentaren des 12. Jahrhunderts," *Biblica* 13 (1932), pp. 61-72, 169-93; "Untersuchung zu den Paulinenkommentaren des 12. Jahrhunderts," *Recherches de Théologie Ancienne et Médiévale* 8 (1936), pp. 253-81.

[66] St. John Chrysostom, *ca.* 354-407, composed 34 *Homilies on Hebrews* which were first issued after his death, from stenographic notes by the Antiochene priest, Constantine. It is an open question in Chrysostom research when and where Chrysostom delivered these sermons (Chrysostomus Baur, O.S.B., *John Chrysostom and his Time*, trans. Sr. M. Gonzaga, R.S.M., Vol. 2 [London, 1960], pp. 94-95). In the sixth century Cassiodorus (d. 563) delegated his friend Mutian, probably a monk, to translate into Latin Chrysostom's *Homilies on Hebrews* ("Opera;" Basel, 1504; *PG* 63. 237-456). We will use Migne's edition of Mutian's translation.

[67] *Von den Konziliis und Kirchen*, 1539, *WA* 50. 519. 22-27. In his *Table Talk* Luther associates his *Lectures on Hebrews* with Chrysostom: "Cum primum legerem epistolam ad Hebraeos, ibi accipiebam Chrysostom eumque legebam, sed er liess mich stecken an allen orten, da ich sein dorfft. Er ist ein lauter wescher, lest den Text fallen; tantum moralia tractat" (*WA Tr* 1. 85. 1-3, Nr. 188, Feb.-March, 1532). "Dum epistolam ad Hebraeos enarrarem et Chrysostomum consulerem, nihil ad argumenta epistolae scripsit. Et credo Chrysostomum, summum rhetorem, habuisse auditorium copiosum, sed sine fructo docuisse" (*WA Tr* 4. 50. 3-6, Nr. 3975, August, 1538).

[68] Riggenbach, p. 11: "Es ist die Grundlage der gesamten abendländischen Auslegungsliteratur zum Hebräerbrief geworden."

Another major source quoted by Luther is the Basel Bible of 1508 with its full apparatus of the interlinear and marginal Gloss, the *Postillae* of Nicholas of Lyra, the *Additiones* to Lyra's *Postillae* by Paul of Burgos and the *Replices* to Burgos' *Additiones* by Matthias Doering.[69] Peter Lombard was responsible for the final composition of the interlinear and marginal Gloss on St. Paul and the Psalms, which he wrote between 1135 and 1136, 1142 and 1143.[70]

Nicholas of Lyra, O.F.M. (d. 1349), is widely acknowledged to be one of the best equipped biblical scholars of the Middle Ages, and an important exegete of Hebrews for Luther. He had an extensive knowledge of both Christian and Jewish exegesis. The importance of Lyra is further attested to by the fact that his *Postillae*, composed between 1322 and 1331, together with the *Glossa ordinaria* and the *Glossa interlinearis* were the classical texts for subsequent exegesis.[71]

Paul of Burgos, O.P. (d. 1435), wrote a critique of Lyra's *Postillae* between 1429 and 1431 entitled *Additiones 1-1100 ad postillam Nicolae de Lyra, Gen.-Apoc.*[72]

---

[69] *Biblia cum Glossa ordinaria, Nicolai de Lyra postilla, moralitatibus eiusdem, Pauli Burgensis additionibus, Matthiae Thoring replicis* (6 vols.; Basel, 1498-1502, 1506-1508); "In Epistolam ad Hebreos," Vol. 6 (Basel, 1508), f. 131r-162v. There are two other editions of the Bible used in the critical apparatus of the new edition (in progress) of Luther's *Dictata super Psalterium: Biblia ... cum concordantiis ... summariis omnium capitum, divisionibus, quattuor repertoriis propositis ... una cum vera nominum Hebraicorum interpretatione* (Basel, 1509); *Biblia cum concordantiis veteris et novi testamenti necnon et iuris canonici, ac diversitatibus textuum, canonibusque evangeliorum ac quibusdam temporum incidentibus in margine positis et accentu singularum dictionum* (Venice, 1511).

[70] Smalley, p. 64. Boendermaker has hung onto the bibliographical legend that ascribed the marginal Gloss to Walafrid Strabo and the interlinear Gloss to Anselm of Laon (Boendermaker, p. 23). In 1949, J. de Blic, in a posthumous article, unmasked the Strabo-Anselm authorship of the *Glossa* as legendary (Smalley, p. 57). The major figures in the composition of the Gloss on St. Paul and the Psalms were, first of all, Anselm of Laon (d. 1117) and, secondly, Gilbert de la Porrée (d. 1154), who expanded Anselm's text. Gilbert's *Media Glosatura* was expanded by Lombard and is known as the *Magna* (or *Maior*) *Glosatura: Super epistolas Pauli glossa ordinaria et magistralis*, in the Basel Bible of 1508 (first published separately in Paris, 1535; PL 192. 399-520).

[71] Herman Hailperin, *Rashi and the Christian Scholars* (Pittsburgh, 1963), p. 138. Lyra, "Epistola Pauli ad Hebreos," *Lyrani Postillae* (Nuremberg, 1493). Lyra's *Postilla moralis* was completed in 1339 and published separately before 1478; thereafter it was usually printed with the *Postilla litteralis*, e.g., Venice, 1588 (Hailperin, p. 142).

[72] Paul of Burgos, O.P., *Additiones* (Lyon, 1490).

Matthias Doering, O.F.M. (1400-1469), defended Lyra's *Postillae* from the criticism of Burgos.[73]

Other commentaries cited by Luther were by three prominent Humanists, Lorenzo Valla (*ca.*, 1406-1457),[74] Jacobus Faber Stapulensis (*ca.*, 1455-1536),[75] and Desiderius Erasmus (*ca.*, 1466-1536).[76]

Secondly, there are two commentators on Hebrews referred to in the critical apparatus of the Hirsch-Rückert and Ficker editions: St. Ambrose and St. Thomas Aquinas.

Luther refers to St. Ambrose twice. In the first instance his knowledge of Ambrose comes by way of Lombard.[77] In the second instance his reference to Ambrose is mistaken probably for Erasmus.[78] Neither Ambrose nor Pseudo-Ambrose (known as Ambrosiaster) wrote a commentary on Hebrews. The commentary on Hebrews that was ascribed in the Middle Ages to Ambrose or Ambrosiaster is actually the work of Alcuin, O.S.B. (730-804).[79] Erasmus apparently was the first to coin the name, Ambrosiaster, as the author of "Ambrose's" commentary on the Epistles of Paul.[80] Luther was exposed to sections of Alcuin's commentary by way of Lombard and probably by way of Pseudo-Hugh of St. Victor, both of whom thought the work to be that of Ambrose.[81] It is worthwhile to work with the commentary of Alcuin because it is the oldest Latin commentary on Hebrews and was used extensively by other medieval commentators on Hebrews.[82]

Ficker refers to St. Thomas' lectures on Hebrews several times.

---

[73] Doering, *Replicam defensivae postillae fratis Nicolai de Lyra ab impugnationibus Domini Burgensis.*

[74] Lorenza Valla, *Adnotationes in latinam Novi Testamenti interpretationem*, ed. Erasmus (Paris, 1505).

[75] Faber Stapulensis, *Epistolae Pauli apostoli* (1st ed.; Paris, 1512; 2nd ed.; Paris, 1515).

[76] Desiderius Erasmus, *Novum instrumentum cum annotationibus* (Basel, 1516).

[77] *WA* 57. III. 116. 9. Cf., HR 118. 22.

[78] *WA* 57. III. 124. 4.

[79] We will use the Migne edition of Alcuin, whose commentary covers chapters 1-10 (*PL* 100. 1031-1084).

[80] Alexander Souter, *The Earliest Latin Commentaries on the Epistles of St. Paul* (Oxford, 1927), p. 39.

[81] Ps.-Hugh cites Ambrose (Riggenbach, p. 19); his commentary on Hebrews was printed before 1500 and probably known to Luther (Alphons V. Müller, "Luthers Lehre in ihrem Verhältnis zu Augustin und zur augustinischen Tradition," *Luther in ökumenischer Sicht*, ed. Alfred von Martin [Stuttgart, 1929], p. 44).

[82] Riggenbach, pp. 19 ff.

Even though Luther does not quote Aquinas' commentary, it is important that it be included in any comparison between Luther and the exegetical tradition because of its influence and the fact that it was read and quoted by later medieval authors—for example, Lyra and Erasmus. Lyra's exegesis, especially his chapter and verse divisions and his outlines of themes, is often very similar to Aquinas' interpretation. Aquinas' *Lectura super Hebreos* occurred between either 1261 and 1264 (P. Mandonnet), or 1265 and 1268 (P. Synave) or 1259 and 1269 (J. M. Vostè).[83]

Thirdly, there are three other commentaries which, for various reasons, are important and merit comparison with Luther. Pseudo-Hugh composed a commentary on Hebrews sometime between 1180 and 1230.[84] This commentary was ascribed in the Middle Ages to Hugh of St. Victor. It was probably known to Luther and, therefore, is important to us.[85]

Another commentary is the work by Petrus de Tarantasia (Innocent V), O.P. (d. 1276). Tarantasia's commentary has been taken to be the work of Nicolas de Gorran, O.P. (d. 1295) because Tarantasia's second redaction was edited under the name of de Gorran.[86] Tarantasia's commentary is important because it often summarizes various positions which had been taken in reference to the exegesis of a verse or passage. It thus gives us sometimes a good survey of the history of exegesis up through St. Thomas.

Another commentary which will be compared with Luther's is that of Dionysius the Carthusian (1402-1471).[87] Dionysius is important for

---

[83] Stegmüller 8064. We will use the Marietti edition: *Super epistolas s. Pauli Lectura,* ed. P. Raphaelis Cai, O.P., Vol. 2 (8th ed.; Rome, 1953), pp. 335-506.

[84] "In epistolam ad Hebraeos," *Quaestiones et decisiones in epistolas divi Pauli, PL* 175. 607-34.

[85] Müller, p. 44.

[86] Tarantasia's first redaction of his commentary on the Epistles of Paul was composed between 1257 and 1262 or 1267 and 1269. It has not been printed or edited, and is on deposit at the following: Berlin, Staatsbibl. Theol. Fol. 14B (Rose 443), f. 1-182: Gal.-Heb.; Cambridge, Univ. 1818 (Ii IV 21) (XIV), f. 1-229. Tarantasia's second redaction, falsely attributed to de Gorran, was printed in Cologne, 1478, The Hague, 1502, Paris, 1531, Antwerp, 1617. For our work we will use the Lyon edition, 1692: "In epistolam b. Pauli ad Hebraeos," *In omnes divi Pauli epistolas enarratio,* Vol. 2 (Lyon, 1692), pp. 160-282.

[87] "Ennaratio in epistolam beati Pauli ad Hebraeos," *Ennarationes piae ac eruditae in omnes beati Pauli epistolas* (1st ed.; Cologne, 1530. "Opera omnia," 13; Monstrolius, 1901), pp. 469-531. We will use the 1901 edition.

this study because of the mystical aspects of his theology. The Doctor Ecstaticus will provide another type of theologian with whom to compare Luther.

Given the preceding exegetes as providing a solid base for getting at medieval exegesis, the following study will examine the extent to which our consideration of Luther's theology is illumined by a comparison with this medieval exegetical tradition. An examination of all the commentaries referred to by Luther as well as those discussed above will provide a broader base for dealing with the medieval exegetical tradition than that circumscribed by Boendermaker. However, in all historical honesty, one should never presume exhaustive discovery and coverage of all exegetical work on Hebrews.

An exception to these principles of selection will be an examination of Augustine. It is an exception for two reasons: One, he did not write a commentary on Hebrews. Two, an understanding of Luther and indeed, the Middle Ages, is impossible without him. Some account, then, of his thought on what emerges as central in medieval exegesis of Hebrews, the relationship between the two Testaments, will be included. It is to be expected that this pivotal figure for medieval and Reformation thought will help nuance the possibilities and the problems. The principle for selecting the Augustine material will be a cross between some of the works Luther cited and the references to *Testamentum* in the 17th century *Concordantiae Augustinianae* (ed. Lenfant).[88] The main Augustine text will be his *Enarrationes in Psalmos* (392-418) because Luther used it in his first *Lectures on the Psalms* (1513-16) and because it covers a large period of Augustine's life.[89]

D. Importance and Intent of Hebrews: The Question of Pauline Authorship

Luther began his *Lectures on Hebrews* with a statement of the importance and purpose of the Epistle to the Hebrews. To one who is more familiar with Luther's later, more critical attitude towards Hebrews, this introduction contains some surprises:

We should note that Paul in this epistle exalts grace and contrasts it with the

---

[88] *Concordantiae Augustinianae sive collectio omnium sententiarum quae sparsim reperiuntur in omnibus S. Augustini operibus*, ed. F. David Lenfant, 2 Vols. (Paris, 1656-65).

[89] *CCSL*, 38-40.

arrogance of legal and human righteousness. He shows that without Christ, neither the law nor the priesthood nor prophecy nor even finally the ministry of the angels was sufficient for salvation. In fact all these were established and provided in reference to the coming of Christ. Therefore, everything considered, he proposes that one should teach Christ alone.[90]

This acceptance of Pauline authorship and thus the importance of the Epistle, by Luther in 1517 is more positive than the vacillating attitude which he had later in his life beginning with the Prefaces to the September Testament of 1522. In this year, in his "Preface to the Epistle to the Hebrews" he expresses his well-known doubts about Hebrews, as well as about James, Jude and Revelation:

> Up to this point we have had [to do with] the true and certain chief books of the New Testament. The four which follow have from ancient times had a different reputation. In the first place, the fact that Hebrews is not an epistle of St. Paul, or of any other apostle, is proved by what it says in chapter 2 [3], that through those who themselves heard it from the Lord this doctrine has come to us and remained among us.

Yet in 1522 he concedes, "one might venture an interpretation" of these texts, but Luther is not sure "that would be sufficient." In 1522 he also says, "it is still a marvelously fine epistle," it "extensively interprets the Old Testament in a fine way," it deals with the Scriptures in "the proper way." "Who wrote it is not known, and will probably not be known for a while; it makes no difference."[91]

In his *Lectures on Hebrews* Luther does not categorically accept the Pauline authorship of Hebrews without discussion of some of the arguments against it. He has some doubts about it, to the extent that he admits that three texts give support to the negative position on Pauline authorship. But he is not nearly as critical as we will shortly see, as is Erasmus in 1516. Before we examine the seven specific texts we will look at the introductions of some medieval exegetes and see what light they shed on Luther's introduction.

---

[90] *WA* 57. III. 5. 10-16: "Notandum in hac epistola, quod Paulus gratiam extollit adversus superbiam legalis et humanae iustitiae, probans, quod sine Christo nec lex nec sacerdotium nec prophetia neque denique angelorum etiam ministerium ad salutem satis fuerit, immo haec omnia in Christum futurum instituta et facta fuerint. Omnino igitur solum Christum docendum proponit."

[91] *LW* 35. 395-96; *WA DB* 7. 344, 631-32.

St. John Chrysostom

In his introduction[92] Chrysostom summarizes the epistle by assuming but explaining Pauline authorship. His question is: "if Paul is not a teacher to the Jews, why did he write to them?"[93] His answer is that while Paul was offensive to his people because of his stand on the law and liberty, nevertheless he had to write to them because he cared so much for them. Furthermore, while it is clear why he was not sent, he was not forbidden to write.[94]

Glossa Ordinaria

There were two general arguments against the Pauline authorship of Hebrews dealt with by medieval exegetes—*modus scribendi* (no salutation or name) and *stilus* (more elegant, different word order and sentence construction than the known Pauline epistles). The Epistle to the Hebrews in the Basel Bible begins with an "Argumentum in epistolam ad Hebraeos," taken by some to have been written by Jerome. The concern of this introduction to the *Glossa* is to deal with *modus scribendi* of the Epistle—the question of why Paul did not sign his name to his letter. The answer is that Paul was writing to the circumcised who regarded him as an apostle to the Gentiles and not to the Jews. Knowing therefore, their pride, and demonstrating his humility, Paul did not want to parade his credentials before their eyes. Paul wrote the epistle in Hebrew, and Luke the evangelist faithfully translated it into Greek after Paul's death.[95]

Pseudo-Hugh of St. Victor

Pseudo-Hugh deals with both *modus scribendi* and *stilus* of Hebrews. In dealing with the argument that Paul's name is not mentioned in the Epistle, he deals with another facet of the argument dealt with in the Bible. Although it is true that Paul, seen to be the destroyer of the law, omitted his name so as not to offend the Jews, nevertheless, was not Paul writing to the converted Jews of Jerusalem to whom the name of Paul must have been most beloved? The answer

---

[92] *PG* 63. 237 does not give Mutian's translation of the "Argumentum," if in fact he translated it, but rather starts with the first Homily.

[93] *PG* 63. 11.

[94] *PG* 63. 13.

[95] *Glossa ordinaria*, f. 131r-131v.

is that to some of these Jews, who claimed that the law as well as grace must be upheld, the name of Paul was odious. Pseudo-Hugh opposes the *stilus* argument by saying that the language of Hebrews is naturally more eloquent because Paul is writing in his own native tongue.[96]

St. Thomas Aquinas

Similarly in his *Prologus*, Aquinas raises the question of Pauline authorship. He reports that before the Council of Nicaea, those who opposed the Pauline authorship of Hebrews did so on the basis of *modus scribendi* and *stilus* of the Epistle and suggested, rather, Luke or Barnabas or Clement as the author. However, an affirmative position was taken by the early doctors of the Church, especially Dionysius the Areopagite and Jerome. Aquinas' defense of Pauline authorship over against the argument of *modus scribendi* is threefold. First, Paul was an apostle to the Gentiles and not the Jews. Secondly, his name was hated by the Jews. And thirdly, he himself was a Jew, and a prophet is not without honor except among his own people. Aquinas' response to the *stilus* argument, like that of the *Glossa* and Pseudo-Hugh, is that the reason the style is more elegant is that Paul wrote the Epistle in his mother tongue and Luke preserved the idiom in his translation.[97]

Nicholas of Lyra

At the end of his *Proemium* Lyra considers the question: "whether this epistle is written by Paul."[98] In opposition to the traditional arguments based on *modus scribendi* and *stilus* of the Epistle, Lyra's response is that without a doubt Paul is the author, for six reasons. The first is the authority of the Church, expressed at Nicaea—the Church alone has the power to determine such matters. The second reason is that the ancient doctors of the Church, especially Dionysius, received it as Pauline. Lyra's remaining arguments are the authority of Chrysostom, the reference to Timothy in the last chapter, Paul's eagerness for the conversion of the Jews and his concern to state the evangelical truth in the face of heresy.

---

[96] Ps.-Hugh, pp. 609-10.

[97] Aquinas, p. 336; cf. Tarantasia, p. 163.

[98] Lyra, f. 133r.

Faber Stapulensis

In his prefatory remarks Faber raises the *modus scribendi* question. He rejects the argument that Paul, the apostle to the Gentiles, omitted a salutation and his name because he was writing to the Jews. For, he says, "who writes a letter without signing his name?" Besides, Paul was writing to fellow believers in Christ, as is clear in chapter 10. Faber rather thinks that the problem originated with the translation from Hebrew into Greek. It is most probable that the translator either had a defective copy or omitted the salutation and started with the main body of the Epistle to which the salutation had been attached.[99]

Erasmus

Erasmus did not preface his commentary with an introduction; however, at the end he adds a long excursus on the subject of the authorship of Hebrews and deals with the traditional questions that had been raised in the introductions of other medieval exegetes. Throughout his commentary Erasmus expresses many reservations about the Pauline authorship of Hebrews. After Hebrews had been accepted into the canon he is probably the first to express serious doubts that Paul wrote it. After a few lines from the beginning, Erasmus says, "Paul, or whoever is the author of the Epistle ...."[100] In the context of 2,7 he says that there is "little probability" that Paul wrote Hebrews.[101] Erasmus in 1516, like Luther in 1522, holds that 6,4-6 denies the possibility of repentance after baptism and, therefore, casts grave doubts on the Pauline authorship of Hebrews.[102]

In his excursus at the end Erasmus concedes that one cannot be certain who wrote Hebrews; yet there are many aspects of the Epistle which indicate that it was not written by Paul. The *stilus* of Hebrews, especially phraseology, differs radically from the Pauline epistles, and it does violence to the Pauline spirit and character. The *modus scribendi*—absence of Paul's name and title—makes it impossible to ascribe authorship to anyone with any certainty. The evidence points to someone other than Paul. For many years, until the time of St.

---

[99] Faber Stapulensis, f. 230v.
[100] Erasmus, p. 585.
[101] Erasmus, p. 586.
[102] Erasmus, p. 590.

Jerome, it was not accepted as Pauline by Rome. But even Jerome
was not certain about the authorship. Ambrose, who commented on
all the Pauline epistles, wrote nothing about Hebrews. Hebrews denies
the efficacy of repentance after baptism, but Paul received into the
communion of saints a man who had slept with his father's wife.
The Epistle seems to defend many heretical teachings.[103] And so
Erasmus ends up very negative on Pauline authorship.

Luther

Luther raises the traditional question of *modus scribendi* in the
context of Heb. 3,7, but comes up with a different defense of Pauline
authorship. He argues that perhaps the reason Hebrews lacks a
Pauline introduction is that Paul knew that he was an apostle to the
Gentiles and not to the Jews. This is similar to the interpretation
of the *Glossa ordinaria*, Aquinas and Tarantasia.[104] However, Luther
adds that Christ himself was the apostle to the Jews and, therefore,
Paul praises Christ alone in his introduction and refrains from praising
himself:

> After Paul has praised Christ the Apostle and his glory, he now begins to urge
> us to have faith in him. Up to this point, in what we could call a prologue, he has
> done nothing else than extol Christ the Apostle, whereas in other epistles he usually
> begins by praising his own apostleship. Perhaps the reason why only this epistle
> is without a personal introduction is that he knew that Christ was the apostle
> and "Servant of the circumcised," as he says here and in Rom. 15, 8, and that
> he, on the other hand, was the apostle and teacher of the Gentiles. Therefore,
> in this epistle it was natural for him to praise the name of Christ, and not his own.[105]

Luther's interpretation of the question of *modus scribendi* is similar
to the emphasis of his introduction. The theme of Hebrews, praise
of Christ, precludes calling attention to any human attainment,
including the apostleship of Paul.

In his Gloss on chapter two, Luther considers the authorship question in relation to Gal. 1, and Pauline phraseology. One of the reasons
Luther rejects the Pauline authorship of Hebrews in 1522 is that
Heb. 2,3 implies that Paul did not receive his authority and gospel
directly from Christ as Paul claims in Gal. 1. Luther's position on

---

[103] Erasmus, pp. 600-601.
[104] *Glossa ordinaria*; f. 131r; Aquinas, p. 336; Tarantasia, p. 163.
[105] *WA* 57. III. 17. 15-22.

Heb. 2,3 versus Gal. 1 in his lectures is that Heb. 2,3 gives strong support to the argument against Pauline authorship because it says that Paul's authority comes from the apostles and shows that he builds on the authority of Mark:

> This text gives very strong support to the argument that Paul is not the author of this epistle, because in Galatians he says and demonstrates that he had received nothing from the other Apostles; furthermore his resource person here is the Apostle Mark (Mark 16, 30).[106]

There was some attempt made by the *Glossa*, Tarantasia, and Dionysius to deal with Paul's use of the word "us" in relation to Galatians.[107] Luther does not harmonize Hebrews and Galatians as they do, and furthermore he holds that 2,3 raises doubts about Pauline authorship.

Luther argues that 2,10 uses a phrase which is unpauline:

> This does not seem to be the characteristic language of Paul. In his other epistles he is not accustomed to say, "through whom," with reference to the Father, but rather, "from whom" or "by whom." He usually says, "through whom," with reference to Christ, as in John 1, 3: "Through whom all things were made." Accordingly Heb. 1, 3, "Upholding all things by the word of his power," refers rather to the Father than to the Son, according to the usual style of Paul.[108]

There is no doubt, however, in Luther's mind that "he, for whom and through whom all things exist" refers to God the Father. Most medieval exegetes agree, but the difference is that many medieval exegetes use the phrase "through whom" in support of their interpretation that the verse refers to the Father, including, in some cases, explicit references to another Pauline epistle.[109]

Luther has many exegetes behind him when he holds that 2,10 refers to God the Father "who makes the author of their salvation perfect through suffering." What is different about Luther's interpretation is his stylistic argument about the customary usage of Paul, compounded by his example of John 1, 3. For stylistically, Aquinas and Tarantasia, referring to Rom. 11, 36, hold that "through whom" is customary Pauline language about the Father. Differing from his predecessors then, Luther claims that 2, 10 refers to the Father in

---

[106] *WA* 57. III. 10. 20-22.

[107] *Glossa interlinearis*, f. 136v; Tarantasia, p. 172; Dionysius the Carthusian, p. 478.

[108] *WA* 57. III. 13. 9-13.

[109] Chrysostom, p. 265; *Glossa interlinearis*, f. 137v; Aquinas, pp. 364-65; Tarantasia, p. 175; Lyra, f. 137v; Dionysius the Carthusian, p. 480; Erasmus, p. 586.

language which is unpauline and thus implicitly casts a shadow on the Pauline authorship of Hebrews.

In the case of both 2, 3 and 2, 10, there is evidence against Pauline authorship.

There are three texts in Hebrews, according to Luther, that contain questionable references to the Old Testament. Heb. 9, 4 says that a "golden censer" was located in the Holy of Holies. In the only section on Pauline authorship in his Scholium, Luther says: "This had led many to hold that this epistle may not have been written by Paul, since Moses never seems to speak of such a censer."[110]

Only Aquinas and Dionysius the Carthusian deal with the apparent conflict. Neither mentions the authorship question.[111]

Luther does not deal with the explanations offered by Aquinas and Dionysius. He offers several arguments to prove the existence of an altar in the Holy of Holies on which the incense was burned. But then he adds:

> I know very well that all these arguments introduced can be easily put aside since the cited texts do not say that there was an altar or censer in the Holy of Holies, but rather outside it and that the high priest should take the incense with burning coals and bring it within the Holy of Holies and burn it there.[112]

Luther simply concludes, without citing the Old Testament, "that there was a censer in the Holy of Holies, because it had a function there and was carried there by the priest during the feast of Atonement.[113]

Heb. 9, 4 also says that in the ark were contained "a golden urn, holding the manna and Aaron's rod." Luther says:

> It is customary to argue further [against Pauline authorship] that I Kings 8, 9 says that there was nothing in the ark except the two tablets of the covenant, whereas the apostle says that there was also a golden urn with manna and the rod of Aaron in the ark.[114]

Aquinas, Burgos, Doering and Faber Stapulensis deal with the apparent conflict between Heb. 9, 4 and I Kings 8, 9. None of them raises the authorship question.[115]

---

[110] *WA* 57. III. 202. 21-22.

[111] Aquinas, pp. 428-29; Dionysius the Carthusian, p. 505.

[112] *WA* 57. III. 203. 24-28.

[113] *WA* 57. III. 204. 5-7.

[114] *WA* 57. III. 204. 8-10.

[115] Aquinas, p. 429; Burgos, f. 152r; Faber Stapulensis, (9, 4) f. 249v; Doering, f. 152r.

Luther, like Burgos, cites Ex. 16 and Num. 17, but draws different conclusions. With regard to the urn and Ex. 16, Luther says:

> It follows from this that, though it is written that there was only manna in the ark, we should not assume that the manna was placed there without its jar (which is what a golden urn is).[116]

Luther holds that Num. 17 does not solve the problem of the rod, but a comparison to the book of Deuteronomy does:

> One could argue with reference to I Kings 8, 9 that when Solomon built the temple he transferred the rod of Aaron from the ark to it. Though there is no text to prove this, it can be demonstrated by a comparison to what happened to the book of Deuteronomy, which during the reign of King Josiah was discovered not against the side of the ark but behind the altar.[117]

Medieval exegetes seem to begin with the assumption that Paul is the author of Hebrews and, therefore, his references to the Old Testament are to be accepted. Luther apparently does not begin with this assumption and therefore, when he discovered that Old Testament support is lacking for a New Testament reference, his conclusion concerns the authorship question. Luther, then, with different arguments from these medieval predecessors, tries to reconcile Heb. 9, 4 with the Old Testament, doing so, in contrast to his predecessors, with an eye to the authorship question.

Heb. 9, 19-21, referring to Ex. 24, describes many details of an incident which are not recorded in the Old Testament. Luther finds no Old Testament basis for most of the items mentioned in 9, 19-21, and thus concludes that the Pauline authorship of Hebrews is questionable:

> Again here the apostle mentions certain items which are not found in the book of Moses. Thus the argument of those who claim that this epistle was not written by Paul is strengthened. Only the following is recorded in Ex. 24, 7-8 by Moses: "Then he took the book of the covenant, and read it in the hearing of the people; and they said, 'All that the Lord has spoken we will do, and we will be obedient.' And Moses took the blood and threw it upon the people, and said, 'Behold the blood of the covenant which the Lord has made with you in accordance with all these words.' " Nothing is said about wool, hyssop, water, the blood of goats, the book, the tabernacle, and the vessels.[118]

Aquinas, observing that there is no reference to goats, water, wool,

---

[116] *WA* 57. III. 204. 17-19.
[117] *WA* 57. III. 205. 4-8.
[118] *WA* 57. III. 52. 19-27.

or hyssop in Ex. 24, presents an explanation which was an interpretation of later medieval exegetes, that Paul is trustworthy because
he was nourished by the law and he knew the use and custom of
the law.[119] Erasmus, poking another hole in the theory that Paul
wrote Hebrews, holds that according to Hebrew, "testamentum"
should read "pactum" or "foedus." Therefore the author of Hebrews
didn't know Hebrew.[120] Luther does not carry on the authorship
question along any of these lines, but simply sees the lack of explicit
Old Testament basis for Heb. 9, 19-21 as a support for the argument
against Pauline authorship. This is the only case of this type in which
Luther does not try to harmonize the Old Testament and Hebrews.
As we will see in the next chapter, he generally sees Hebrews as a
guide to the Old Testament.

Heb. 12, 21 attributes a statement to Moses during the giving of
the law which is not explicitly in the Old Testament. Although this
raises the authorship question for Luther, he argues that this statement is implicitly a part of the incident of the burning bush and
the dividing of the Red Sea.

> This statement of Moses is nowhere recorded in Scripture. Thus, this has been
> an argument for those who deny that this epistle was written by Paul. But on
> a similar occasion, according to Ex. 3, 6, Moses was terrified when he lay flat
> before the bush and was afraid to look at God. And in Ex. 14, when the Lord was
> about to divide the Red Sea, he said to Moses: "Why do you cry to me?" (Ex.
> 14, 15). Therefore it is quite likely that Moses trembled here also. However, it
> is not recorded because of his office as legislator, so that it would not be said that
> the giver of the law was terrified by the law.[121]

Aquinas offers two explanations of the discrepancy between 12, 21
and the Old Testament. Perhaps, he says, Paul is actually referring
to the incident of the burning bush in Ex. 3 where it says that Moses
was afraid. Or, perhaps Paul is drawing upon a document that is
no longer extant.[122] Tarantasia, Lyra, and Dionysius the Carthusian,
like Aquinas, hold that Ex. 3 is the background for Heb. 12, 21.[123]
Faber Stapulensis argues that the discrepancy arose with the trans-

---

[119] Aquinas, p. 436; Tarantasia, pp. 230-31; Lyra, f. 151r; Dionysius the Carthusian,
p. 507; Faber Stapulensis (9, 20), f. 249r.

[120] Erasmus, p. 593.

[121] *WA* 57. III. 83. 11-17.

[122] Aquinas, p. 491.

[123] Tarantasia, p. 269; Lyra, f. 160r; Dionysius the Carthusian, p. 525.

lator of Hebrews who misunderstood Moses' statement in Ex. 20, 20 ("Do not fear") to be a reference to Moses himself.[124]

Erasmus claims that there is nothing in Ex. 3 or 20 to support the statement attributed to Moses in Heb. 12, 21:

> I suspect that this is the place to which Jerome refers when he says that some do not attribute this epistle to Paul because it quotes certain things with reference to the Old Testament which are not to be found there.[125]

Luther, therefore, sides with those medieval exegetes who hold that Ex. 3, 6 is background material for Heb. 12, 21. However, he alone adds the explanation that perhaps Moses also trembled during the Red Sea incident, but it was not recorded "so that it would not be said that the giver of the law was terrified by the law." Luther also raises the authorship question as does Erasmus. But Luther does not go as far as Erasmus regarding this verse and see it as clear evidence against Pauline authorship.

In the matter of these references in Hebrews to particulars of the Old Testament, Luther, with one exception, comes out positively on the question of Pauline authorship.

The last instance in his Gloss where he raises the authorship question concerns the question of Paul's imprisonment (13, 19). Luther says: "This verse is an argument in favor of the Pauline authorship of Hebrews since it connotes bondage and imprisonment."[126]

Valla, in the context of another verse (10, 34: "For you had compassion on the prisoners"), argues that the verse speaks of Paul's imprisonment and therefore "proves that this epistle is Paul's, since he says, 'You had compassion on my chains;' he does not say, you had compassion on the prisoners."[127] Erasmus (on 10, 33) counters that this reasoning is frivolous if not ridiculous because many of the successors to the apostle experienced imprisonment.[128]

Luther does not comment on 10, 33-34, but, like Valla, argues in a different context (13, 19) that reference to imprisonment is a definite argument in favor of Pauline authorship.

In these seven instances then, where Luther raises the authorship question, he is generally in favor of Pauline authorship. The reverse

---

[124] Faber Stapulensis, f. 259r.

[125] Erasmus, p. 599.

[126] *WA* 57. III. 91. 17-18.

[127] Valla, p. 887.

[128] Erasmus, pp. 594-95.

side of the coin is that in most instances he does even raise the question. Erasmus, on the contrary, frequently and sometimes caustically deals with the question with negative conclusions. Luther, however, does not automatically presume Pauline authorship, and so when there is a question about the relationship of Hebrews to the Old Testament, he deals with it. He is not content to rest the case with traditional answers to the questions of *modus scribendi* and *stilus*. The importance of Hebrews is that Paul has something to say about Christ and the Old Testament.

CHAPTER TWO

THE RELATIONSHIP BETWEEN THE TWO TESTAMENTS

It is next our task to look more closely at the importance and purpose of Paul's Epistle to the Hebrews as presented in medieval commentaries. Medieval exegetes of Hebrews as well as Luther announce in their introductions and throughout their analyses that the decisive theme of Hebrews concerns the relationship of Christ to the Old Testament. As to how this theme is understood in the exegetical tradition we will consult the major developments of medieval exegesis of Hebrews, namely, Chrysostom and Alcuin, *Glossa interlinearis* and *ordinaria*, Aquinas and Lyra, Faber and Erasmus. In order to gain a more complete understanding of medieval discussions of the relationship between the Old and the New Testaments, Augustine will be examined. With a more nuanced understanding of medieval interpretations we will look at Luther to see what light these medieval discussions shed on his theology of Christ and the Old Testament. First we will look at Luther's *Lectures on Hebrews* and then we will relate Luther's interpretation of 1517-18, to his earlier biblical commentaries in order to gain a more complete understanding of his thought and of his relationship to medieval theology.

A. MEDIEVAL EXEGESIS OF HEBREWS AND ST. AUGUSTINE

St. John Chrysostom

Chrysostom announces in his introduction and repeats in almost every Homily that Paul's purpose in writing to the Jews is to show the relationship of Christ (New Testament) to the Old Testament. Paul makes "frequent reference" (*crebra mentio*) simultaneously (*simul*) to the Old and New Testaments. The reason Paul dwells so extensively on the two Testaments simultaneously, is "ad resurrectionis persuasionem." The use of the Old Testament is to provide additional evidence for the *excellentia Christi*.[1] Paul executes his purpose slowly

---

[1] *PG* 63. 14.

in order not to lose his readers. In his very first Homily, on Heb. 1, 1,
the contrast between "olim" and "novissime diebus istis" means for
Chrysostom the *eminentia* of the New Testament period over the
Old and the superiority ("superiores") of Christians over the Jews—
we have "multo amplius."[2] And yet that God spoke through the
prophets and later through his Son does not quite establish the
superiority. The real question is "unde ostendis *nostri* [emphasis mine]
temporis eminentiam?" To have said simply, "God has spoken
through his son," all Paul would have shown was that the Old and
New Testaments were "of one and the same." Thus, to show "the
excellence of our time," Paul added "nobis."[3] The comparative
contrast between the two time periods really means that "God has
spoken *to us* in his Son."

The comparison of the Testaments, resulting in the excellence of
the New in contrast to the Old, is continuous from the beginning
in Chrysostom, even though Paul is supposedly soft-pedaling it at
the start. Chrysostom uses the comparative frequently: "superius,"
"melior"; the comparison results in "maxima differentia";[4] even
though "et illa praecepta et ista" are of God, "sed non similiter. Et
hoc quidem postea demonstrat"; "See how he [Paul/Chrysostom]
makes the comparison";[5] "secundum comparationem" of Christ and
Moses, Paul is "already [in Heb. 3, 1] sowing seeds of *excellentia*
[*Christi*]."[6]

In order to show "how much better the New Testament is than
the Old,"[7] the category is *eminentia* (*excellentia*), and the method is
secundum comparationem.

The difference between the Testaments for Chrysostom is the
"comparative excellence" of the New. The "eminentia" or "excellentia" of Christ is a relative matter. For example, the fact that Christ
is "superior" to the high priests of the Old Testament means that
there are some similarities between them as well as some differences:

> He points out first the things which are common [to Christ and the high priests],
> and then he shows that Christ is superior. For comparative excellence means

---

[2] *PG* 63. 237.

[3] *PG* 63. 238.

[4] *PG* 63. 252.

[5] *PG* 63. 255-56.

[6] *PG* 63. 273.

[7] *PG* 63. 290.

that they share certain things in common and that in other matters he excels: otherwise it is not a matter of comparison.[8]

The comparative *excellentia* or *differentia*, clearly stated to be Paul's main purpose in Homily XII on 7, 1ff., is also described by Chrysostom in terms of the relative likeness (*simile/dissimile*) between *typus* and *veritas*. There is enough likeness for purposes of comparison.[9] The category and pattern of comparison is basic, even within the Old Testament itself. The superiority of Christ over Melchisedec is intensified by Chrysostom's arguing the superiority of Melchisedec over Abraham, of priesthood over promise: "Thus the type of Christ is better even than he who had the promises."[10] Comparison is radical to the category of Testament. Christ as priest, is superior to the superior of the Old Testament.

The change from Old to New Testament necessitated a change in the priesthood. "If another priesthood is introduced there must also be another testament, because a priest cannot be without a testament, without a law, nor without precepts."[11] Testament is a priestly category associated with law.[12] Since the priesthood is changed, so is the Testament. There are two distinct, but comparatively related, Testaments.[13]

Chrysostom strongly influenced the exegesis of Hebrews for the next six centuries, as can be seen in Alcuin, who throughout his commentary is heavily dependent on Chrysostom's *Homilies on Hebrews* in Latin translation. He begins his *Commentary on Hebrews* with a summary of the Epistle. Paul's primary intent in this Epistle is to bring his own people to the Christian faith and to "distinguish between the eminence of grace given through the Son and the shadows of the law given through angels."[14]

St. Augustine

The starting point for our examination of Augustine will be his *Enarrationes in Psalmos* (392-418). Other writings of his will be con-

---

[8] *PG* 63. 291.
[9] *PG* 63. 316-18.
[10] *PG* 63. 318.
[11] *PG* 63. 322.
[12] *PG* 63. 341-45. Cf. Homily XVI.
[13] *PG* 63. 323.
[14] *PL* 100. 1031.

sulted as various aspects of his understanding of the two Testaments emerge from the *Enarrationes*.

One aspect of Augustine's understanding of the relationship between the two Testaments that comes up early in his *Enarrationes* is that there are two eras in the divine plan of salvation covered by the two Testaments.

In Ps. VI, he distinguishes between "two generations," one "pertains" *ad corpus*, the other *ad animam*. The first, from Adam to Moses, is "carnal," "exterior," "the old man to whom the Old Testament is given." The second, from the coming of Christ, is "the transition from circumcision of the flesh to circumcision of the heart," "interior," "the new man and the New Testament."[15]

In Ps. VII, "the strength of the New Testament" bends and breaks the *duritia* of the Old Testament.[16]

In Ps. XXXIV, Augustine stresses the providence of God over everyone and everything, temporal and eternal. Like a doctor he knows who needs medicine and who doesn't, better than the patient. *Ergo* "he divided the times of the Old and New Testaments." Their promises are for things terrestrial and celestial respectively, but the commandments for worshipping God and living rightly are the same in each.[17]

The promises of the two Testaments differ, and so too their *hereditates*. *In Ps.* LXVII, Augustine considers the text, "Si dormiatis inter medios cleros," and the interpretation of *cleri* as the two Testaments.[18] The text and *Testamentum* have a strong *inter* characteristic. *Testamentum* is "inter se et populum," "inter me et te," and "between themselves they ought to have *consensum*," "lest they disagree with each other."[19] If we were to understand *cleri* as *Testamenta*, the text, to sleep between the Testaments, would mean we should not interfere with the Testaments consenting between themselves and with their *concordia*. Linguistically, Augustine prefers that *cleri* be understood as the *hereditates* of the Old and New Testaments, which are temporal felicity and immortality. This means to live *in spe* of the heavenly inheritance and to rest from desiring temporal felicity.[20]

---

15 *CCSL* 38 (VI, 2), 28. 8-48.
16 *Ibid.*, (VII, 14), 45. 2-4.
17 *Ibid.*, (XXXIV, S. 1, 7), 304. 11-24.
18 *CCSL* 39 (LXVII, 17-20), 879-83.
19 *Ibid.*, (LXVII, 19), 881. 6-882. 28.
20 *Ibid.*, (LXVII, 19-20), 882. 30-883. 17.

In Ps. LXXIII, Augustine sets the distinction between the two Testaments in the context of divine purpose and management (*dispensatio*).[21] We must separate (*discernimus*) the two according to their different sacraments and promises, never forgetting however, that in the divine plan God is *creator* and *auctor* of both Testaments.[22] The commandments are the same. The reason for the two Testaments is that man is first "animale," second, "spirituale." Man is first *puer*, and thus is given first *puerilia* and *ludicra*. So you give your son a rattle when he is young and a book when he is grown up.[23] (In contemporary western society the process is exactly reversed).

The difference between Old Testament and New Testament sacraments and promises is again, the difference between *terrena* and *caelestia*. The Old sacraments promise a savior, the New give salvation. To describe the change, Augustine uses the comparative. The New are "faciliora, pauciora, salubriora, feliciora."[24]

Above, Augustine described *testamentum* in rather bilateral terms: *inter. In Ps.* LXXXII, he also defines *testamentum* as an agreement *inter*, as a *pactum* and *placitum*: "*Testamentum* to be sure, is used in the Scriptures not only to refer to that which is only validated by the death of the testators, but every *pactum* and *placitum* they called *testamentum*."[25]

In the covenant there is real strength (*magnum firmamentum*) in God's "I will."[26] On account of Christ the *testamentum* is *fidele*. Christ is *mediator, signator, fideiussor, testis, hereditas, coheres*.[27] The *testamentum* is *immobile* because God has predestined his heirs and will not go back on his word.[28]

In the divine economy there are the two eras and the corresponding two Testaments. There is also "testamentum aeternum," (Ps. 104, 10) which cannot refer to the Old Testament because it is abolished by the New. The *testamentum aeternum* is *testamentum fidei* or *testamentum*

---

[21] *Ibid.*, (LXXIII, 2), 1005. 1-1007. 60.

[22] *Ibid.*, (LXXIII, 2), 1006. 40-41.

[23] *Ibid.*, (LXXIII, 2), 100W. 3-4.

[24] *Ibid.*, (LXXIII, 2), 1006. 25-26.

[25] *Ibid.*, (LXXXII, 6), 1142. 3-5.

[26] *Ibid.*, (*In Ps.* XXXVIII, S. II, 2), 1233. 9.

[27] *Ibid.*, (*In Ps.* LXXXVIII, S. I, 28), 1232. 2-6.

[28] *Ibid.*, (*In Ps.* LXXXVIII, S. II, 4), 1236. 24-26.

iustificationis et hereditatis aeternae, "which God has promised to faith."[29] Within the two Testaments and during the time covered by them and since, there is the one and eternal *testamentum dei* available to faith.

In his other writings, Augustine also emphasizes that the two Testaments cover two eras in the divine economy, each with their distinct characteristics and purposes. In his anti-Manichaean writing, he is, of course, more concerned to defend the Old Testament against Manichaean attacks on it and to emphasize the unity and harmony of the two Testaments. He does however, deal with the differences between the two within the *dispensation* of the one God. In his *Contra Adimantum* (early anti-Manichaean) the *differentia* is between *onera servorum* and *gaudia liberorum, praefiguratio* and *possessio,*[30] or, most succinctly, "timor et amor."[31] In *De vera religione* (anti-Manichaean, 390), Augustine uses the models of medicine and *pater familias* to argue against those who deny that both Testaments (one *minor*, the other *major*) are from the same God. Such a position would have to hold that it would not be possible for a *iustissimus pater familias* to adjust his laws depending on whether he was dealing with servants or sons, or for a single physician to prescribe one type medicine to weaker patients through his assistants, and another to stronger patients by himself. The *ars* and *pactum medicinae* remain committed to *salus*. Medicine is geared to the state of health: "ita divina providentia."[32]

One aspect of Augustine's understanding of the relationship between the two Testaments is (a) that they cover the development of God's providence for his people as the needs of their health dictated; (b) that *testamentum*, like *pactum* denotes an *inter* relationship; (c) that the two eras have different sacraments and promises (*terrena/caelestia, timor/amor*) and the comparative describes the difference; and which leads us to the second aspect, (d) that within the two Testaments, from the beginning to the end of the world, there is the one *testamentum fidei*.

We return to *Enarr. in Ps.* to consider a second aspect of Augustine's

---

[29] *CCSL* 40 (*In Ps.* CIV, 7), 1539. 1-12.

[30] *CSEL* 25 (16), 163. 15-26.

[31] *Ibid.*, (17), 166. 28.

[32] *CCSL* 32 (XVII, 34), 208. 23-41.

understanding of the relationship between the two Testaments. We have already seen that for Augustine, in the divine *dispensatio* there is the one *testamentum dei*. He is the author and creator of his providence. God, through his word confronts his people with a sword sharpened on both sides.[33] He speaks of things temporal and eternal. The blow accomplishes its purpose: to separate from the world, to promise the eternal and fulfill the temporal. The two sides of the sword represent the two Testaments. "In each the *sermo dei verax* as a two-edged sword is found."[34]

So for Augustine, there is not a simple identification of Old Testament = *terrena*, New Testament = *aeterna*, though in providential categories we have found this distinction. The two-edged *sermo dei* is found in both Testaments. To apply Augustine's sanative metaphor, not all the patients need the same medicine at the same time. There is one *testamentum* and *sermo dei*.

The one *sermo dei*, "found in each Testament," is found differently— hidden in the Old, revealed in the New. *In Ps.* LXVII, in the context of the providential "fullness of time," the grace of the New Testament is hidden (*latet*) in the Old until it was pleasing to God to reveal his Son.[35] In the "dregs of the corporeal mysteries" of the Old Testament, "Novum Testamentum absconditum latet."[36] Circumcision, the Temple, the land of promise, the sacrifices, each is a *res* of great mystery.[37] "In vetere Testamento figurabatur Testamentum Novum."[38] What God was doing in the Old Testament is clear in the New: "Vetus Testamentum in novo revelatum, in Vetere Novum velatum."[39] The one *testamentum* is *velatum* in the Old Testament, *revelatum* in the New.

Some understood what God was doing, thus "belonging already to the New Testament which is the kingdom of heaven," even though they were living during the time of the Old Testament. Renewed by grace, some put off the old and put on the new.[40] The categories of old and new man do not completely coincide with Old and New Testament.

---

[33] *CCSL* 40 (*In Ps.* CXLIX, 12), 2185-86.

[34] *Ibid.*, (CXLIX, 12), 2186. 36-37.

[35] *CCSL* 39 (LXVII, 33), 893. 7-13.

[36] *Ibid.*, (*In Ps.* LXXIV, 12), 1033. 27-28.

[37] *Ibid.*, (LXIV, 12), 1033. 29-1034. 37.

[38] *Ibid.*, (*In Ps.* LXXXIV, 4), 1163. 4-5.

[39] *CCSL* 40 (*In Ps.* CV, 36), 1567. 9-10.

[40] *CCSL* 38 (*In Ps.* XXXII, S. II, 8), 253. 1-7.

In his other writings Augustine also distinguishes three parts of what we are calling "a second aspect" in his understanding of the relationship between the two Testaments: (a) one God, and thus one testament; (b) *velatum/revelatum*; (c) not everyone in the Old Testament was old, nor then, was everyone in the New Testament new; some in the Old belonged to the New. Of course, all these parts and aspects are interrelated.

In the *Contra Adimantum* Augustine adduces texts from both Testaments to show that they agree and are both written by one God.[41] In *De moribus ecclesiae catholicae* (anti-Manichaean, 388), he says succinctly, "Utriusque Testamenti Deus unus est."[42]

The *velatum/revelatum* distinction between the two Testaments is in the context of the divine plan of the one God of both Testaments. In the *Contra Faustum* (anti-Manichaean, 398), Augustine argues that the Old Testament contains figures and *praenuntiationes* of the New Testament.[43] The hope of a future world with *iustitia* and *immortalitate*, "which hope we have in Christ," was hidden (*occultatum*) in the Old Testament *in figura*, revealed (*revelatum*) in the New Testament *in manifestatione*. This divine schema was understood by some saints in the Old Testament.[44] In his *Ad Honoratum* (anti-Pelagian, 412), Augustine says the New Testament "was figuratively foreshadowed" in the Old Testament, which belongs (*pertinet*) to the old man and the earlier stages of the world. Those few saints who understood this "made known the Old Testament in accordance with the time," yet they belonged (*pertinent*) to the New.[45]

The *occultatum/revelatum* distinction is an *et...et* relationship: both the New is concealed (*latet*) in the Old, and the Old is made clear (*patet*) in the New.[46] "The same things, to be sure, are in the Old and the New, there concealed, here revealed, there prefigured, here made clear."[47]

Though there are two *magna Testamenta*,[48] the New is hidden in

---

[41] *CSEL* 25 (7), 130. 4-8.

[42] *PL* 32 (XVII, 30), 1324.

[43] *CSEL* 25, (IV, 2), 269. 4-12.

[44] *Ibid.*, (VI, 9), 300. 19-301. 1.

[45] *CSEL* 44 (Epistola 140 II, 5), 158. 6-25.

[46] *CCSL* 33 (*Quaestionum in Heptateuchum*, 419-20, Liber secundus, Quaest. Exodi LXXIII), 106. 1277-80.

[47] *Ibid.*, (Liber quartus, Quaest. Numerorum XXXIII, 1), 255. 768-71.

[48] *CCSL* 48 (*De civitate dei* XVI, 27), 532. 11.

the Old and is a *revelatio* of the Old.[49] During the ages of the world
before Christ, some (few) patriarchs, prophets, and saints understood
the *testamentum hereditatis sempiternae*. The progression in fulfilling
the law is the development from desiring things temporal to things
spiritual. These few desired the spiritual reward.[50]

Membership in the Old or New does not coincide in every case
with those who lived during the ages before and after Christ or in the
Old and New Testaments. In the *De baptismo contra Donatistas* (400),
one "belongs" to the Old or New Testament by virtue of commitment
or "desire." Those before Christ who did not see the spiritual in the
earthly and desired only earthly promises belonged (*pertineo*) to the
Old Testament.[51] "At any time," therefore, those who have a "taste,"
"hope," or "desire" for things carnal are *animales*. By the time of
Moses, the Old Testament was manifest and the New "hidden" in
it. In Christ, the New is revealed. "Just as in the sacraments of the
Old Testament some saw the Spirit, belonging secretly to the New
Testament which was then concealed, so too now in the sacraments
of the New Testament which has already been revealed many live
who are *animales*, and if they will not advance to receive the things
of the Spirit of God...they will belong to the Old Testament."[52]

At any time there are those who belong to the Old (flesh) and
those who belong to the New (spirit). The Old Testament/New Testament dichotomy then, transcends the time boundaries of the Old and
New Testaments.

Along the same lines of discussion about the relationship of the
two Testaments is Augustine's *Contra duas epistulas Pelagianorum
(ad Bonafacium)*.[53] The stewards (*dispensatores*) and bearers (*gestatores*)
of the Old Testament are heirs of the New Testament because they
understood the "ordering of the times."[54] The *iusti* and *sancti* before
Abraham up to John the Baptist are sons of promise and grace,
heirs of God and coheirs of Christ.[55] All *iusti* before Christ, even
Moses—*minister* of the Old, *heres* of the New,—belong to the New
Testament because they (as we) believed in the incarnation, passion,

---

49 *Ibid.*, (XVI, 26), 531. 62-63.
50 *CCSL* 46 (*De catechizandis rudibus* XXII, 39-40), 163-165.
51 *CSEL* 51 (I, XV, 23), 167. 23-168. 2.
52 *Ibid.*, (I, XV, 24), 168. 3-30.
53 *CSEL* 60 (III, IV, 6-13), 492-501.
54 *Ibid.*, (III, IV, 6), 492. 6-9.
55 *Ibid.*, (III, IV, 8), 494. 12-17.

and resurrection of Christ.[56] They, not *nomine* but *re*, were Christians by the same grace of the Holy Spirit.[57] They belong to the Old Testament who receive the *sanctam bonam* and *iustam* law as letter and as sufficient as letter.[58] The Old Testament is described "distinctius vetus instrumentum quam vetus testamentum." It is the *ministerium Moysi*.[59] The Old Testament is called "old" because it was revealed (not instituted) in an earlier time and the New Testament "new" because it was revealed (not instituted) later.[60] The New Testament was made clear and confirmed through the blood of Christ.[61] The two Testaments, beyond the boundaries of the two eras and the two books, become the pattern for the development of the man of faith. "The Old Testament then, belongs to the old man, from which it is necessary to make a beginning, the New Testament to the new man, to which a man ought to pass from his old state."[62] Not everyone in the Old Testament is old, nor everyone in the New Testament new. God progressively reveals his plan of salvation, first rather secretly in the Old Testament, then openly in the New. Some understood in the Old and belonged to the New. Some in the New did not, and belonged to the Old. Since the time of the two Testaments (as well as during it), the progression from old to new is the model for everyman to put off the old and hold in faith to *spiritualia*.

In this "second aspect" of Augustine's understanding of the relationship between the two Testaments we have seen (a) that they are of one God, (b) whose plan of salvation is *velatum* in the Old and *revelatum* in the New, and (c) that the Old Testament/New Testament dichotomy transcends the time boundaries of the two books and becomes a model for the development of the man of faith—old man becoming new man.

On a strictly hermeneutical level, Augustine's understanding and interpretation of the two books is governed by a principle of the harmony between the two. This has been implicit in and would follow from the two aspects already discussed. In the *Contra Adimantum* he uses the phrase, *concordia utriusque testamenti*, to describe their

---

[56] *Ibid.*, (III, IV, 11), 497. 16-21.

[57] *Ibid.*, (III, IV, 11), 498. 6-9.

[58] *Ibid.*, (III, IV, 9), 495. 1-2.

[59] *Ibid.*, (III, IV, 12), 498. 13-22.

[60] *Ibid.*, (III, IV, 13), 500. 1-4.

[61] *Ibid.*, (III, IV, 9), 495. 24-25.

[62] *Ibid.*, (III, IV, 13), 500. 30-501. 3.

relationship.[63] In terms of things praised and preached the texts of the two Testaments agree completely.[64] In the *concordia* of both Testaments it becomes quite clear what one's moral conduct ought to be.[65] In his *De utilitate credendi* (anti-Manichaean, 392) he argues that *secundum analogiam* the *congruentia* of both Testaments is clear.[66] The *congruentia* of the two Testaments is so great that there is no point (*apex*) at which they don't agree.[67]

The first two aspects of Augustine's understanding of the Testaments is more his understanding of the historical realities covered by the books—the divine *dispensatio*, the two *hereditates* of the one God, the one *testamentum fidei* first *velatum* then *revelatum*, etc. This third aspect or level of Augustine's thought on the subject concerns more Augustine's hermeneutic as theologian dealing with contemporary theological and polemical issues, most notably of course, the Manichaean and Marcionite denunciation of the Old Testament. Augustine's understanding and use of Scripture when polemicizing and/or exegeting and/or whatever, is based on the hermeneutic of the *congruentia* of the two great Testaments. These three have been isolated for purposes of clarification, but in Augustine's day-to-day work they are quite interrelated.[68]

This account of Augustine, as of others, is geared to a better understanding of Luther and as a Luther study will hopefully contribute to contemporary historical scholarship. Though not its intention, this rather nuanced account of Augustine may lead to a better contemporary understanding of him. A brief assessment of some contemporary scholarship would indicate that well it might. The earlier coverage of the material by Pontet is basic and extensive, but seems to lack

---

[63] *CSEL* 25 (4), 123. 27-28; (7), 128. 9.

[64] *De moribus ecclesiae catholicae, PL* 32 (XVI, 27), 1322.

[65] *Ibid.*, (XVIII, 34), 1325.

[66] *CSEL* 25 (IV 3, 7), 9. 5.

[67] *Ibid.*. (3, 9). 13. 20-22.

[68] *Contra adversarium legis et prophetarum* (anti-Marcionite, 420): "Unde et fides venturi Christi habitabat utique in Prophetis, venturum praenuntiantibus Christum; et nunc sunt plurimi carnales, qui vel haereses faciunt non intelligendo Scripturas, vel in ipsa Catholica aut adhuc parvuli lacte nutriuntur, aut tanquam palea perseverans futuris ignibus praeparantur. Sicut autem Deus unus et verus creator bonorum est et temporalium et aeternorum, ita idem ipse auctor est amborum Testamentorum; quia et Novum in Vetere est figuratum, et Vetus in Novo est revelatum." (*PL* 42 [XVII, 35], 623).

a critical edge.[69] The studies by de Lubac, Strauss and Preus seem to be limited to the hermeneutical statements and level of Augustine's work. De Lubac shows that in the thought of several Fathers, including Augustine, the phrase, "diversi, sed non adversi," well describes their understanding of the relationship of various parts of Scripture to one another. But on other levels we have seen that Augustine's understanding of the two Testaments could well be described as *diversi et adversi*.[70] Strauss concentrates on the unity and various "senses" of Scripture.[71] Preus is limited to the hermeneutical statements of method in two works of Augustine. The "confusion" Preus sees might have been helped if he had seen Augustine's hermeneutic in practice and thus, considered the following: (1) the *dispensatio* doctrine, (2) the sanative motif, (3) the hermeneutical divisions within the Old Testament and within the New Testament, and (4) *testamentum fidei*.[72]

The various aspects then, of Augustine's understanding of the relationship between the two Testaments which we have found in his *Enarrationes in Psalmos* and several other works are as follows: There are two eras and two great Testaments under the providence of one God. The doctor (*pactum medicinae*) has provided different promises and sacraments. *Inter* God and his people the commandments are constant. But the New sacraments and promises are *salubriora* because of Christ, the *signator* of the one *testamentum dei* (*testamentum fidei*).

The instrument of providence is *sermo dei verax*, a two-edged sword, present in both Testaments and always present to separate *spiritualia* from *temporalia*. The *sermo* is *velatum* in circumcision, the Temple, and other *temporalia*, *revelatum* in Christ. Those (men of faith) who separate *spiritualia* from *animalia* "belong" (grow up) to the New, those who regard the *lex bona* to be sufficient as letter "belong" to the Old. Fulfilling the law is the process each must undergo by turning away from the temporal and "desiring" the spiritual *hereditas*. The object of all medicine is *salus*. "At any time" the *testamentum iustifi-*

---

[69] Maurice Pontet, *L'Exégèse de S. Augustin Prédicateur* (Paris, 1944).

[70] Henri de Lubac, "À propos de la formule: Diversi sed non adversi," *Recherches de Science Religieuse* 40 (1952), pp. 27-40.

[71] Gerhard Strauss, *Schriftgebrauch, Schriftauslegung und Schriftbeweis bei Augustin* ("Beiträge zur Geschichte der biblischen Hermeneutik," Vol. 1; Tübingen, 1959).

[72] James S. Preus, *From Shadow to Promise: Old Testament Interpretation from Augustine to the Young Luther* (Cambridge, 1969).

cationis is at work. Those who "understand" are *re* Christians by the one Holy Spirit.

Hermeneutically, because of one author, all parts of Scripture, including the two great Testaments, are in complete *congruentia*.

Glossa Interlinearis et Ordinaria

The *Glossa ordinaria* begins with a statement of the purpose and content of Paul's Epistle to the Hebrews. Paul's intent in relation to the Hebrews was to show the "eminentia Christi" and the "sufficiency of faith," and to compare it with the "insufficiency and uselessness of the law." Comparison between the two Testaments is made to show how preferable the New is to the Old: Christ to the prophets, Christ to the angels, Christ to Moses. Christ is *maior*. The New Testament is preferable to the Old because the law is *umbra*, and Christ *veritas*.[73]

The model for comparison is a developmental model seen in each of the Testaments themselves. In the *Prothemata in omnes Pauli epistolas* the relationship of the epistles to the Gospels is discussed. It is like the relationship of the prophets to the law: *sub velamine* in the law, *apertius* in the prophets.[74] In reference to Heb. 5, 1, Paul wishes to show that "novum melius veteri testamento." Certain things are common and certain other things are "better" in the New Testament. Certain "altiora" pertain to Christ alone, certain "humiliora" pertain to Old Testament priests alone.[75] While there is development, the emphasis, as in Chrysostom, is on "differentias." Because " a priest cannot exist without a testamentum, law and precepts," the " translatio" of the priesthood means a "transeundum" from law to gospel,

---

[73] *Biblia cum Glossa ordinaria* f. 131v: "Primum proponit audienda esse verba Christi conferendo eum prophetis, quia in eo locutus est Dominus ut in prophetis; et maior est eis. Deinde commendat eum alternatim secundum utramque naturam humanam scilicet et divinam. Postea comparat eum angelis et praefert, multa interserens de excellentia eius secundum utramque naturam. Deinde comparat eum Moysi et praefert. Deinde multis rationibus et auctoritatibus gratiam fidei umbrae legis preferendam declarat. Et sacerdotium Christi Levitico sacerdotio; et testamentum novum veteri eiusque sacrificium unum multis illius sacrificiis praeponendum ostendit, quia ibi umbra, hic veritas. Tandem ponit fidei descriptionem, eam multis testimoniis commendans. Circa finem vero moralem subdit instructionem." Cf. f. 135v, 139r.

[74] *Ibid.*, n. f.

[75] *Ibid.*, f. 141v.

from Old Testament to New Testament.[76] The "hermeneutical divide" (Preus) is between the Testaments.

Even though God gave the Old Testament, it is "destroyed" and "substituted" by the New Testament, because its *status* is *infirmum* and now, "post adventum Christi," *inutile*. The useless things given through the Old Testament were given *ad significationem* to the New Testament.[77] "Ad differentiam testamentorum" shows "how much better Christ and his law is." His *ministerium* is *melius*.[78] As in Augustine, for the *Glossa* the precepts in both Testaments are "the same," but the ceremonies, sacraments, and promises are not. In Hebrews, "Paul proves that the testament of Christ is better than the Old Testament."[79] The reason why we do not worship God by the same rite that the fathers of the Old Testament did is that "God has given us another rite through the fathers of the New Testament. This is not contrary to the Old Testament because it was already foretold there."[80] Then the *Glossa* tells us "to consider diligently the difference between the two Testaments: Old and New." The Old is letter which kills, the New spirit that vivifies. The reason why we hold to the authority of that Testament whose rites we do not observe is that "it is necessary that the same things are read and received lest we destroy the prophets." Some things are such *in instrumento veteris testamenti* that we observe them; those which we do not are not damned but fulfilled.[81]

Although there is development within each Testament, basically the development is between the two Testaments, and that development is Christ. After the advent of Christ the Old Testament is useless except to lend "credibility" to the New Testament. "The distinction between the Old and New Testaments, in which not only the sacraments but also the promises differ, is the passion of Christ."[82] The comparison between the two Testaments is necessary to show that the New surpasses the Old as well as transforms it.[83]

---

[76] *Ibid.*, f. 145v-146r.
[77] *Ibid.*, f. 146r.
[78] *Ibid.*, f. 147v.
[79] *Ibid.*, f. 148r.
[80] *Ibid.*, f. 148r.
[81] *Ibid.*, f. 148r.
[82] *Ibid.*, f. 150v.
[83] *Ibid.*, f. 149r.

St. Thomas Aquinas

"The theme which distinguishes the Epistle to the Hebrews from the other Epistles is *excellentia Christi*" says Aquinas in his "Prologue" to his lectures on Hebrews.[84] Paul's concern to demonstrate the superiority of Christ means that he intends to show the "excellentia Novi ad Vetus Testamentum per excellentiam Christi." The intent of the theme of *excellentia Novi Testamenti* is to show Jewish converts that Christ is "preferable" to the angels, law and priesthood of the Old Testament. The praise of Christ in the New Testament—his *origo, dominatio, operatio* and *dignitas*—shows that the New Testament is greater in every respect than the Old.[85]

The theme of *excellentia* or *eminentia Christi* is developed by a "comparison" of the two Testaments.[86] The New Testament is compared, and shown to be preferable to the Old in many ways. The *locutio* in the New Testament is "more perfect."[87] Christ is "greater than the angels,"[88] "more excellent than Moses,"[89] "more excellent than the priests of the old law,"[90] and "a minister of greater and better sacraments than those of the old law."[91] The result of the comparison is that Christ is *excellentior* than the old law,[92] and "Novum Testamentum est excellentius quam vetus."[93]

Integral to the comparison of the two Testaments is a discussion of their *differentiae*.[94] An important *differentia* drawing from Augustine, is *timor* and *amor*. The Old Testament is "lex timoris" whereas "love is in the New."[95] The metaphor of light and darkness is also used.

---

[84] Aquinas, *Super epistolas s. Pauli lectura*, p. 335.

[85] *Ibid.*, p. 337.

[86] *Ibid.*, pp. 357, 425, 444, 489, 493.

[87] *Ibid.*, p. 338.

[88] *Ibid.*, p. 357.

[89] *Ibid.*, pp. 372, 374.

[90] *Ibid.*, pp. 389, 419.

[91] *Ibid.*, p. 421.

[92] *Ibid.*, p. 389: "Sicut a principio huius epistolae dictum fuit intentio Apostoli est ostendere Christum excellentiorem esse omnibus his ex quibus lex habet auctoritatem, scilicet angelis, quorum ministerio data fuit, Gal. III, 19: 'Ordinata per angelos,'— et Moyse, qui fuit legislator, Io. 1, 17: 'Lex per Moysen data est,'—et sacerdotio et pontificatu Aaron, per quem lex administratur."

[93] *Ibid.*, p. 436.

[94] *Ibid.*, pp. 369, 427, 438.

[95] *Ibid.*, pp. 369, 423, 489-91.

Characteristic of the old law is *nox* and *umbra*, whereas the new law dispels the darkness and brings *dies*.[96] In the Old Testament there were only *figuralia* but in the New is the *veritas figurarum*.[97] In the New Testament the *mundatio* is *melior* and *perfectior*.[98] Another contrast is the difference between the ways they were given. The Old Testament was transmitted "per exteriora," the New Testament was given "interius."[99] In whatever manner the two Testaments are set side by side, the result is the same. The New is *melius, perfectius, excellentius*.[100]

The basis of the comparison of the two Testaments for Aquinas, is the category of *lex. Testamentum* and *lex* are interchangeable terms when he deals with the two eras and books. The Old Testament is *lex timoris*, the New Testament is *lex amoris*.[101] The "same precepts" exist in both Testaments. Aquinas draws on the *Glossa* when he says "a priest cannot be without a testament, law and precepts."[102] Since the New Testament is so much better than the Old, the *doctrinae* and *mandata* of Christ in the New Testament ought to be obeyed so much more.[103] God, the author of both Testaments,[104] had a divine plan appropriate to the times. The "carnal precepts" were appropriate to *pueris, ante adventum*, to point to the future coming. The "spiritual precepts" were given to *perfectis, post adventum*, to refer to the advent of Christ.[105] The law and tabernacle of the New Testament is an interiorization of the Old.[106]

The origin and authority of law is dealt with in one place in terms

---

[96] *Ibid.*, p. 374.

[97] *Ibid.*, p. 423.

[98] *Ibid.*, p. 438.

[99] *Ibid.*, p. 424.

[100] *Ibid.*, p. 422: "Item in illo dicuntur quaedam, quae pertinent ad cultum Dei, et ista sunt caeremonialia: quaedam vero, quae ad rectitudinem vitae, et ista sunt praecepta moralia, quae manent: alia vero, non. In Novo autem adduntur consilia illis praeceptis, quae dantur perfectis, qui sunt capaces spiritualium. Et sic manent praecepta eadem, sed promissa diversa. Item sacramenta sunt diversa; quia ibi erat figura tantum, hic autem figurae veritas expressa. Per omnia ergo testamentum illud est melius."

[101] *Ibid.*, p. 442.

[102] *Ibid.*, p. 413.

[103] *Ibid.*, p. 357.

[104] *Ibid.*, p. 340.

[105] *Ibid.*, pp. 414-15.

[106] *Ibid.*, p. 433.

of Moses and Christ and the giving of the law.[107] Aquinas holds that Moses is only "promulgator" of the law, whereas Christ is "legislator principalis." Christ is the true giver of the law, and "as lawgiver built the Church." Moses however, is "quasi legislator," and only as "legis pronunciator" deserves praise. So again, Christ is preferable to Moses and ought to be obeyed accordingly. The category for the ministry of both Moses and Christ is the same: *legislator.*

The Old and New Testaments divide at *adventum Christi.* "The origin of the New Testament" is twofold—Christ and the apostles. The "initium enarrationis" (Heb. 2, 3) "happened in time through the Word incarnate." The *origo* of the teachings of the New Testament then, began in time with the advent of Christ.[108]

The giving of the Testaments in time is understood by Aquinas in terms of the organic metaphor of development. Certain things *de Christo* are prefigured in the Old Testament through, e.g., David and Solomon. This is so because the things of Christ—his *origo, dominatio, operatio* and *dignitas*—are of such magnitude, power and splender that they could not be introduced *subito*: "The things of Christ are so great that they would not have been believed unless they had first been disseminated gradually through the growth of time."[109] The development in time from Old Testament to New Testament is the development from imperfect to perfect, so that the New Testament is "perfectius."[110] The model of development seen in the comparison of the two Testaments includes the relationship of the "present Church" to the "glory of heaven." As the Old Testament is a *figura* of the New, so the New Testament and the Church is a *figura* of heaven. The Old Testament than, is a "figura figurae."[111] The model of development and the category of *figura* is understood in terms of clarity—clarity of *mandata, doctrina,* and *de bonis futuris.* In the development of the Testaments, the New Testament is *expressius.*[112] Or, as he says in his *Summa Theologiae* ("De comparatione legis novae ad veterem"), the New Testament is contained in the Old Testament as a tree in its seed: *quae credenda,* are "handed over"

---

[107] *Ibid.,* pp. 371-73.
[108] *Ibid.,* pp. 357-59.
[109] *Ibid.,* p. 338.
[110] *Ibid.,* p. 339.
[111] *Ibid.,* p. 428.
[112] *Ibid.,* p. 442.

(*trado*) in the New Testament *explicite et aperte*, but in the Old Testament *implicite sub figura*.[113]

For Aquinas then, the dominant motif of Hebrews is *excellentia Christi et Novi Testamenti*, a theme comparative in nature—"New is said only in comparison to Old."[114] By showing what the two Testaments have in common and wherein they differ, Aquinas concludes that the *multo excellentius*[115] means the New is *melius, perfectius, expressius*. The continuity of the two Testaments and the base of their comparison is *lex* and the figure of *legislator*. The two Testaments divide in time with the advent of Christ. The divide marks the development from seed to tree, Old to New. Christ transforms *lex timoris* into *lex amoris*.

Nicholas of Lyra

Lyra agrees with Aquinas, the *Glossa interlinearis* and the *Glossa ordinaria*, Alcuin and Chrysostom, that the main theme of the Epistle to the Hebrews is the *eminentia Christi*, that is, the *eminentia Christi* "with reference to" and "by comparison with" the Old Testament:

> Therefore in this epistle Paul shows the eminence of the New Testament with reference to the Old, showing that the Old is compared to the New as disposition to form and as imperfection to perfection. The imperfect passes away and ceases to exist with the coming of the perfect, as in I Cor. 13, 10: ["When the perfect comes the imperfect will pass away."][116]

The conclusion that Lyra draws from this comparison is that the New Testament is "excellentius et efficacius veteri."[117]

The perfection of Christ's Testament in relation to the Old is demonstrated in three ways. First of all, it is shown from the perspective of the inadequacies of the Old. The Old is shown to be imperfect with reference (*respectu*) to the New.[118] The Old (Mosaic) law is imperfect *de fide*. The doctrines of the trinity and incarnation were not

---

[113] *ST*. I—II, 107. 3c and *ad* 1.

[114] Aquinas, *Super epistolas s. Pauli lectura*, p. 425.

[115] *Ibid.*, p. 335.

[116] *Biblia cum Glossa ordinaria*, f. 133v: "Et ideo in hac epistola ostendit eminentiam novi testamenti respectu veteris, ostendens quod vetus comparatur ad novum sicut dispositio ad formam, et sicut imperfectum ad perfectum quod evacuatur et cessat adveniente perfecto, ut dicitur 1 Cor. 13 [10]."

[117] *Ibid.*, f. 150v.

[118] *Ibid.*, f. 131v.

"explicitly" developed in the Old Testament. But it is natural in the development of knowledge to begin with "minor things" before "the truth" is revealed. The "body of the law or its commandments" were also imperfect because they regulated "only exterior acts" and "insufficiently" at that. The moral, ceremonial, and judicial laws all were imperfect. The "finis" of the old law was imperfect because it was "obscure" and "shadowy."[119] So, from the perspective of its teaching, precepts and purpose, the old law was incomplete.

A second perspective or theme is the perfection of the New Testament with reference to the Old. The "evangelical law" is perfect in every respect that Lyra considered the old law to be imperfect:

> Secondly, the perfection of the evangelical law is touched on first and foremost in the words: "That which is perfect." And it is clear that its perfection is to be compared with the imperfection of the law because it is perfect with reference to the knowledge of faith, the precepts and the goal of the law. In these things the Mosaic law was imperfect.[120]

The perfection and excellence of the New Testament is arrived at from three directions: *ex tempore* ("olim" vs. "novissimis"), *ex legislatore* (angels vs. Son), *ex modo tradendi* ("obscure" vs. "lucide et aperte").[121]

Throughout his commentary Lyra works out the details of the comparison between the two Testaments. Chapters 1 and 2 show that Christ "preeminet" the angels, while chapters 3 and 4 demonstrate that he "excellit" Moses.[122] In chapters 5 ff., reiterated in chapters 7 through 9, Paul shows that the priesthood of Christ "preeminet" the priesthood of Aaron, with the result that Christ is seen to be *excellentior* than the priesthood of the Old Testament.[123] The levitical priesthood ceases with the coming of Christ just as *umbra* does with the coming of *veritas* or imperfection with the coming of perfection. "And in the same manner the old law ceases with the coming of the new because law and priesthood run *pari passu*."[124] In each instance,

---

[119] *Ibid.*, f. 131v-132v.

[120] *Ibid.*, f. 132v: "Secundo principaliter tangitur in verbo proposito perfectio legis evangelice cum dicitur: 'Ad quod perfectum est.' Et patet eius perfectio comparando eam ad legis imperfectionem, quia perfecta est respectu cognitionis fidei, et respectu preceptorum, et respectu finis in quibus lex mosaica erat imperfecta."

[121] *Ibid.*, f. 133v.

[122] *Ibid.*, f. 138v.

[123] *Ibid.*

[124] *Ibid.*, f. 146r.

Lyra re-emphasizes that Paul's concern is to demonstrate the *excellentia Christi respectu* the Old Testament or some aspect of it. In other words, the New Testament is perfect in every way that the Old was not.

The third aspect of the relationship between the Testaments is the *ordo* of the two Testaments or laws. The relationship is that " 'when the new comes the old passes away' (I Cor. 13, 10)."[125] There are three aspects to the *ordo* of the two laws. In the "order of time, the old law is prior to the new." There is also an "order of dignity" and an "order of virtue," which show that the New Testament is "prior" to the Old.

The Old Testament "passes away" in various ways.[126] In one way, as in the case with ceremonial laws, the old law is made completely void. With regard to the moral law of the Old Testament, Lyra holds that its imperfection is discarded. This claim of Lyra as well as his statement that the new law is "perfect with reference to" its "precepts," whereas the old law was imperfect,[127] is different from Aquinas' emphasis that the "same precepts" exist in both Testaments. For Aquinas the moral precepts of the Old Testament remain in force in the New Testament as well as the new laws added to the old.[128]

---

[125] *Ibid.*, f 132v.

[126] *Ibid.*, f. 132v-133r: "Considerandum tamen quod diversimode evacuantur precepta moralia legis et cerimonialia et iudicialia. Ad cuius intellectum sciendum, quod quando fit mutatio a contrario in contrarium, oportet terminum a quo totaliter evacuari, sicut quando ex albo fit nigrum, albedo tollitur. Quando autem ex imperfecto fit perfectum, non tollitur totaliter terminus a quo, sed tantum eius imperfectio, scilicet, quando ex minus albo fit magis album non tollitur albedo precedens, sed tantum eius imperfectio. Ulterius considerandum, quod quando corrumpitur terminus a quo per accidens illud quod est ei adiunctum corrumpitur, potest tamen manere cum termino ad quem si non habeat ad ipsum contrarietatem, non tamen manet numero, sed specie tantum, sicut quando de aere fit ignis, manet qualitas symbola. Cerimonialia igitur evacuantur primo modo, quia contrariantur novae legis cultui.... Moralia autem precepta evacuantur tantummodo secundum quid, scilicet, quantum ad imperfectionem.... Et sic patet quod moralia precepta veteris legis non evacuantur quantum ad substantiam legis, sed solum quantum ad imperfectionem. Propter quod dicit apostolus i. Cor. xiii. 'Cum factus sum vir, evacuavi quae erant parvuli.' Status autem veteris legis comparatur puero, secundum quod habetur Gal. iii.a. 'Lex pedagogus noster fuit'; pedagogus autem est ductor pueri. Status novae legis comparatur viro perfecto; et ideo sicut manet idem homo quantum ad substantiam in pueritia et virili aetate, remota tantum imperfectione pueritiae, sic est de moralium preceptorum evacuatione. Iudicialia autem precepta evacuantur tertio modo, quia adveniente lege gratiae, cessat eorum obligatio."

[127] *Ibid.*, f. 132v. Cf. Burgos' opposition to, and Doering's defense of Lyra on "translatio" of the moral law. (f. 146r-146v).

[128] Aquinas, p. 422.

For Lyra the relation between the moral precepts of the old law to the precepts of the new law is that of "disposition" to "form," "imperfection" to "perfection," "boy" to "man," "off white" to "pure white" and *terminus a quo* to *terminus ad quem*. The old law for Lyra is the basis of the new—the old moral law "does not pass away as to substance" but "as to imperfection."[129]

The old law "passes away" differently again with regard to the judicial laws. They are invalidated in the sense that their specific commandments no longer have any obligatory force. Yet they may have functional and symbolic value if they are obeyed from the motive of love and not fear.[130]

The two Testaments, for Lyra, are radically different, though necessary for the development of human understanding. The two Testaments divide at the time of Christ, the Old ceasing and the New beginning. The Old is the testament of law, the New the testament of gospel. Paul's Epistle to the Hebrews is "prima in ordine doctrinae" because he shows that the imperfection of the law ceases in the time of perfection which is the time of Christ.[131] The theme of *excellentia Christi* is developed by Lyra to emphasize the total contrast between the Old and New Testaments.

Lyra emphasizes more the contrast between the two Testaments than does Aquinas. Aquinas stresses more the development and continuity of the two Testaments. They say many of the same things. For example, both say the development is from imperfect to perfect. Aquinas concludes that the New is *perfectius*. Lyra does not, and leaves the comparison with the contrast between imperfect and perfect.

Faber Stapulensis

Faber, like others we have studied, holds that the theme of Hebrews is *excellentia Christi*.[132] Comparative in nature this theme means that the New Testament is "more excellent" than the Old. Christ is *praestantior*, which means he is *excellentior, potior, augustior*.[133] Or, in another place, Faber says that Christ is *melior, maior, superior*.[134]

---

129 *Ibid.*, f. 133r-133v.

130 *Ibid.*

131 *Ibid.*, f. 131v.

132 Faber Stapulensis, *Epistolae Pauli apostoli*, f. 230v.

133 *Ibid.*, f. 230v.

134 *Ibid.*, f. 242v.

> The New Testament is as much more excellent than the Old, as the Son of God is superior to Moses. It is as much more excellent as the promises of the New are more important than those of the Old.... There is a vast difference between the promise of heaven and the promise of Canaan.[135]

Although the excellence of Christ is comparative in nature, because "when one says the New Testament, the Old Testament immediately comes to mind,"[136] the comparison of the two Testaments for Faber means the New is radically new, and the Old radically old. He emphasizes more the great difference between the two Testaments. The comparison of darkness and truth is prominent, and compared to the light of truth, darkness is nothing:

> Between Moses and Christ there is a vast chasm of difference.... He who places his confidence more in Moses than in Christ confides more in darkness than in truth. The truth excels darkness and is as much more powerful as a lord is more powerful than a servant, as being than non-being, as God than a creature. When the light comes the darkness vanishes and is nothing. Thus compared with Christ Moses is nothing. Of such light is the pre-eminence of Christ.[137]

The commandments of Moses have been broken—"so also the Old Testament was to be broken and abolished." The commandments of the New Testament remain.[138] The old law is the law of *carnalia*, the new of *spiritualia*. "The old law was not simply law but a beginning of law, a type, a beginning of the perfection of works. Therefore when the law of perfection was brought in, the old law is cast aside, i.e., rendered useless and void."[139] The Old Testament is "aged," "decayed," "destroyed" with the coming of Christ.[140] In fact, the "Old Testament was not so much testament as it was shadow (*umbra*) of the Testament."[141] *Umbra* he defines as *rudis adumbratio*.[142] The

---

135 *Ibid.*, f. 246v.

136 *Ibid.*, f. 246v.

137 *Ibid.*, f. 234r: "Sed inter Mosen et Christum: latum est differentiae intervallum.... Ergo qui in Mose confidunt: in umbra confidunt. Et qui in Mose plus confideret quam in Christo; in umbra plus confideret quam in veritate, quae tanto praecellit et efficacior est umbra: quanto dominus servo, immo quanto ens non ente et Deus creatura. Et ut umbra, adveniente luce, vanescit et nihil est: ita si ad Christum confers nihil est Moses; tanta luce est Christi praeeminentia."

138 *Ibid.*, f. 242r.

139 *Ibid.*, f. 242v.

140 *Ibid.*, f. 246v-247r.

141 *Ibid.*, f. 248v.

142 *Ibid.*, f. 250v.

Old Testament contains *typus, figura, mysteria* of the New Testament.[143] The heroics of faith on the part of some Old Testament patriarchs (c. 11) are a figure and example of all those who, following Christ, receive life and salvation.[144]

Everything changed radically with *tempus adventus Christi* which was *tempus emendationis, correctionis, rectificationis.* "Christ changed everything for the better, indeed, for the best."[145]

The New Testament is new relative to the Old Testament. Compared to the Old Testament however, the New is completely new, and the Old completely old. The discontinuity marked by the coming of Christ is radical. Both are under the category of law; the Old is dead and the New perfect and eternal. For the Christian, the only continuity is hermeneutical—the old book contains figures and examples of the real thing.

Erasmus

Erasmus does not deal with any general theme(s) or purpose(s) in the Epistle to the Hebrews.[146] His only general concern in the heavily philological "Annotationes" is with the question of Pauline authorship, and that question is basically of philological interest to him. Elsewhere[147] I have shown that, during this time, Erasmus is very critical of the Old Testament. He regards the people of the Old Testament to be superstitious, cruel, barbarous, and sexually perverse by comparison with the ancient civilizations of Greece and Rome and their *bonas litteras.* At one point he was willing that the Old Testament should be altogether abolished. His understanding of the two Testaments is governed by his hermeneutic of *philosophia Christi* contained in the New Testament.

Conclusion

We have seen from our study of the major exegetes of Hebrews that they agree as to the central themes of Paul's epistle: *excellentia Christi* vis-à-vis Jewish converts (Chrysostom, *Glossa* [Lombard],

---

[143] *Ibid.*, f. 248r.

[144] *Ibid.*, f. 255r.

[145] *Ibid.*, f. 248r.

[146] Erasmus, *Novum instrumentum cum annotationibus.*

[147] "From Testament to Covenant in the Early Sixteenth Century," *The Sixteenth Century Journal* 3 (April, 1972), pp. 6-7.

Aquinas, Lyra, Faber). We briefly noted that Alcuin agrees with Chrysostom, and we could draw on other exegetes of Hebrews, for example, Petrus de Tarantasia,[148] Paul of Burgos,[149] and Dionysius the Carthusian[150] to further substantiate the thesis that the exegetical tradition as a whole gives *excellentia Christi* as the controlling theme. There are differences as to how this theme is developed and nuanced.

We have also seen from these same exegetes that the theme of *excellentia Christi* means a comparison between the Old and New Testaments. The conclusion of the comparison is that Christ's testament is *excellentius*. Again, as to how the relationship between the two Testaments and the comparative are understood and nuanced, there are differences.

These differences tend to polarize around an emphasis on continuity or on discontinuity between the Testaments. Chrysostom and *Glossa* point out development within each Testament but emphasize the contrast or discontinuity between the two Testaments, which is also the emphasis of Lyra, Faber, and Erasmus. Aquinas on the other hand, emphasizes the development or continuity between the two Testaments. Augustine seems to have confused everything: he discusses development within and between, continuity and discontinuity within and between. This is because Augustine's position is quite different from the others.

All figures discussed agree on a providential and hermeneutical level, that there are two distinct but somehow related Testaments (eras and books). It is on this level that the metaphors of doctor-*salus*, boy-man, seed-tree, imperfect-perfect, etc., are used to show that the two Testaments are appropriate for natural maturation. Man comes to see and understand gradually. The model is organic development and the category for this is clarity—relatively and/or absolutely clearer understanding of revelation. It is also on this level that the contrasts of *temporalia/aeternalia*, *umbra/veritas*, *timor/amor*, *velatum/revelatum*, etc. are used to describe the characters and relationships of the different eras and books. There is complete hermeneutical congruence and one God is author of both eras.

---

[148] Tarantasia, "In epistolam b. Pauli ad Hebraeos," *In omnes divi Pauli epistolas enarratio*, pp. 163, 179, 216.

[149] Burgos, *Additiones*, f. 136r.

[150] Dionysius the Carthusian, "Enarratio in epistolam beati Pauli ad Hebraeos," p. 469.

Augustine's position is different on a soteriological level, where the emphasis is on the contrast between the two testaments (flesh and spirit) within each Testament (era and book). The exegetes of Hebrews with whom we have dealt locate the distinction between the two Testaments at *adventus Christi*. Augustine also distinguishes between the two testaments in terms of the individual's "belonging" to the Old or to the New. For Augustine soteriologically there is one *testamentum fidei*, one *sermo dei verax*, and the difference between the testaments lies in man's decision. Soteriologically, the two testaments are a model for the development of faith.

We have also noted that *testamentum* is a sacerdotal and legal term. The New Testament is a new law. Christ is new *legislator*. Law and priesthood keep equal step (Heb. 7, 12), so a change in priesthood necessitates a change in testament. Christ is greater than Melchisedec (priest) who in turn is greater than Abraham (promise). It is the person of Christ as priest that transforms the old law.

Both Testaments are law, and commandments exist in each. The authors discussed differ as to the precise relationship between the old (especially moral) law, and the new. Augustine, *Glossa*, and Aquinas emphasize that the commandments are constant. Chrysostom, Lyra, and Faber emphasize the discontinuity between the two sets of laws. In either case, the new law is better than the old.[151]

B. Luther, Lectures on Hebrews

Luther begins his *Lectures on Hebrews* with a brief statement of its content and purpose:

> We should note that Paul in this epistle exalts grace as opposed to the arrogance of legal and human righteousness. He shows that without Christ, neither the law

---

[151] This conclusion adds another dimension to our general understanding of the medieval concept of law and gospel. On the basis of sermonic and academic works, Heiko A. Oberman has shown that Gabriel Biel, in accord with traditional medieval academic theology, taught that "*whether Old or New, both Testaments fall in the same category: Lex,*" and both their dispensors fall in the category of *Legislator* (*The Harvest of Medieval Theology: Gabriel Biel and Late Medieval Nominalism* [Cambridge, 1963], p. 119). The medieval academic or systematic tradition held that the two laws differ only in degree. The law of Christ fulfilled and perfected the law of Moses by "the interiorization of righteousness" (*Ibid.*, pp. 112 ff.). In its interpretation of Hebrews the medieval exegetical tradition gives Oberman's treatment of "the medieval tradition" (*Ibid.*, p. 119) a broader base of support.

nor the priesthood nor prophecy nor even finally the ministry of the angels was sufficient for salvation. In fact all these were established and provided in reference to the coming of Christ. Therefore everything considered, he proposes that one should teach Christ alone.[152]

Luther's introduction deviates greatly from medieval introductions to Hebrews by not discussing and developing the traditional theme of *excellentia Christi* compared with the angels, Moses and the priesthood of the Old Testament. Rather than use the comparative theme of *excellentia Christi*, Luther tells his students that Paul in Hebrews singles out *gratia* and *Christus* and opposes (*adversus*) them to the law, priesthood, prophecy and angels prior to the coming of Christ. Paul, reports Luther, intends to teach Christ alone—period. One senses that "Omnino," ("everything considered") and "solum" ("alone") have a polemical thrust over against the medieval exegetical tradition. The final sentence could also read: "only Christ at all," "Christ alone no matter what," "Christ alone no matter how you slice it." Whereas medieval exegetes in general held that Paul in Hebrews was concerned to demonstrate that Christ is "more excellent" than the old law, Luther seems to be saying that Christ cannot be compared on the same level with anyone or anything, that the differences between Christ and the law, priesthood, prophecy and angels is not a matter of degree. Although Chrysostom and others emphasize the contrast and discontinuity between the Testaments, Chrysostom, for example, says "they share certain things in common and in other matters Christ excels, otherwise it is not a matter of comparison." The varying emphasis on continuity or discontinuity by the medievals is based on the law as a common level for comparison or contrast. Luther has shifted the base of comparison. Only Christ suffices for salvation in each era or Testament.

Like Augustine, Luther sees the relationship between the two Testaments as a soteriological problem. Augustine also considered the relationship in what we have called hermeneutical and providential categories. It seems that Luther sees the relationship solely in soteriological terms.

---

[152] *WA* 57. III. 5. 10-16: "Notandum in hac epistola, quod Paulus gratiam extollit adversus superbiam legalis et humanae iustitiae, probans, quod sine Christo nec lex nec sacerdotium nec prophetia necque denique angelorum etiam ministerium ad salutem satis fuerit, immo haec omnia in Christum futurum instituta et facta fuerint. Omnino igitur solum Christum docendum proponit."

Research on Luther's *Lectures on Hebrews* gives us little help at this point in determining Luther's understanding of testament and of the relationship between the two Testaments—a problem which provides perennial matter for discussion for serious biblical, historical, and systematic theologians. In Luther studies however, Boendermaker is the only scholar who gives any significant consideration to this problem. He does not appear, though, to recognize its importance in Luther's *Lectures on Hebrews*, either in themselves, or in their relation to medieval exegesis and Luther's own previous exegesis. In fact, Boendermaker finds both similarity and contrast between Luther and medieval exegetes on the question of testament.[153] In a discussion of Law and Gospel Boendermaker simply says that for Luther, the Old and New Testaments are not related to each other as time-periods of wrath and grace. For in the Old Testament also we find expression of God's mercy.[154]

While the relationship between the two Testaments (*excellentia Christi*) was the major preoccupation of medieval exegetes of Hebrews, it remains to be seen what understanding of the relationship Luther has, and what importance he attaches to the problem.

Luther's opening Gloss to chapter 3 appears to be traditional:

> After the apostle has praised the excellence of Christ, which is that he was made higher than the angels, he now proceeds to teach that one should extol Christ in preference to Moses, whom the Jews assigned the highest place below the angels. His purpose, therefore, is to remove their trust even in Moses and direct them to Christ alone.[155]

---

[153] It is difficult to see how Boendermaker, in his comparison of Luther and Lyra, could claim that the following quotation from Luther and Lyra show "important agreement:" LU: "gratiam extollit adversum superbiam legalis et humanae iustitiae." LY: "ostendit eminentiam novi testamenti respectu veteris." (Boendermaker, p. 27). In pointing out a difference between Luther and Lyra on Law and Gospel, Boendermaker misreads *comparatio* (of the two testaments) in Lyra (Lyra, f. 160r.) as *cooperatio* (Boendermaker, pp. 69, 78).

[154] Boendermaker, p. 78.

[155] *WA* 57. III. 15. 18-21: "Postquam Christi commendavit excellentiam, qua angelis melior effectus est, iam prona sequela eum praeferendum docet Mosi, de quo Iudei summam post angelos habebant opinionem, ut sic etiam Mosi fiduciam ab eis tolleret et in solum Christum converteret." Lyra makes the following statement with regard to the same loci: "UNDE FRATRES, etc. [Luther's comments are made with regard to UNDE] Postquam apostolus declaravit excellentiam novi testamenti respectu veteris per hoc quod praeeminet Christus angelis, hic consequenter ostendit hoc idem per hoc quod excellit Moysen." (Lyra, f. 138v.). Boendermaker does not mention this parallel (Boendermaker, p. 34).

The traditional elements seem to be the following: the phrase *excellentia Christi*, use of the comparative, and the word "prefer" (*praeferendum*). Luther uses the phrase *excellentia Christi* only here and in one other place.[156] Here the phrase *excellentia Christi* goes with the following phrase, "who was made higher than the angels." But actually this latter phrase is a quotation from Heb. 1, 4. This fact is not indicated in the *Weimarer Ausgabe*. The sentence ought to read, therefore, as follows: "After the apostle has praised the excellence of Christ, which is that 'he was made higher than the angels'...."

Luther is traditional in that he understands the phrase *excellentia Christi* to be comparative in nature. Christ is greater than the angels. The thrust of his interpretation, however, is not traditional because he does not develop or use the theme, *excellentia Christi*. Nor, secondly, does he capitalize, as did his medieval predecessors, on the comparative phrases in the Epistle. Hebrews uses the comparative with regard to the relationship between the two eras in nine places: 1, 4; 2, 1; 3, 3; 7, 22; 8, 6; 9, 11; 9, 23; and 12, 24. In his glosses on these texts he, as is the nature of a gloss, paraphrases the comparatives and thus often repeats the comparative with reference to the two eras. But in his Scholium, where his own particular exegetical and theological concerns are evidenced, the case is different. In six out of the nine cases Luther does not comment at all on the verse in his Scholium. Though in three cases he does comment on the verse, in two cases (7, 22 and 9, 23), he does not comment on the comparative, but on some other aspect of the verse. In the only instance where Luther does deal with the comparative in a verse from Hebrews (9, 14), he does so in order to show how "opposite the purity (*munditia*) of the old and new testament is"—the opposites are shown "per antitheses."[157] Note that the concern is soteriological.

Finally, Luther's use of the word "prefer" is colored by the phrase, "Christ alone." In other words, only Christ is to be chosen. There is absolutely no basis for comparison between him and anyone else.

Luther's opening gloss to chapter 3, therefore, is similar to his introduction. Only Christ counts for salvation. The traditional type of introduction is lacking as well as the traditional significance of the phrase *excellentia Christi*, the comparative degree and the word

---

156 *WA* 57. III. 188. 18-19.

157 *WA* 57. III. 207. 9-10: "Diversam munditiam novi et veteris testamenti pulchre describit et per antitheses deducit."

"prefer." Luther sees the two testaments as antithetical ways of salvation.

As one works through Luther's *Lectures on Hebrews*, he soon notices that Luther stresses the differences and contrasts between the two testaments: "He magnifies and places before their eyes the difference between the two testaments."[158] With reference to Heb. 2, 2, Luther says that the law was "valid" only in an "external" way.

> Therefore, to fulfill the law is an act of pure hypocrisy which really weakens it, [the law] because the will of the heart sets its goal on something radically different than the law, namely, on punishment or reward.... This is the case with every man who is outside Christ.[159]

Luther continues in his exegesis of the next verse (2, 3), by saying that law and gospel "also differ" with respect to the way of salvation: "Law and gospel differ also because the law requires many works which are all external, but the gospel requires one work which is internal, and that is faith."[160]

In his Scholium on 3, 1, Luther contrasts the law and the gospel with reference to the way they are presented: "Roaring language pertains to the law," whereas "a soft current of air," the gospel, "ought to be presented gently to the terrified and the humiliated."[161]

In fact, in his gloss on 7, 1, Luther explicitly says that Paul's purpose up to this point "has been to underscore repeatedly the difference between the old and the new testament."[162]

The clue to the understanding of the relation between the law and the gospel in his *Lectures on Hebrews* is to be found in his Scholium on Heb. 7, 12, which reads: "Once there is a change in the priesthood, there is a change in the law as well." Luther says that this word "law" can have a double meaning. The "inferior understanding"[163] is that "law" refers to ceremonial laws only.[164] The "superior understanding" interprets law in the sense in which Paul uses the word in his Epistles to the Romans and Galatians, namely, as "everything

---

158 *WA* 57. III. 82. 22-23.
159 *WA* 57. III. 113. 13-18.
160 *WA* 57. III. 113. 21-23.
161 *WA* 57. III. 136. 22-28.
162 *WA* 57. III. 36. 8-11.
163 Cf. Burgos, f. 147r.
164 *WA* 57. III. 190. 16-25.

that is prescribed by God and man, be it ceremonial, judicial, or moral."[165]

Thus for Luther the gospel has completely and totally replaced the law, be it the ceremonial, judicial, or moral law. The gospel of the new testament ("the redemption of Christ") is not merely by virtue of degree better than the law of the old testament. It is completely other.[166] The gospel has replaced the law as the fundamental category of Christian theology.

Luther's understanding of Hebrews and of the relationship between the two testaments differs fundamentally from his predecessors. For them the new era is a similar/dissimilar, but in any case a natural development beyond the old—better, more excellent. For Luther there is not development but absolute antithesis, soteriologically, between the testaments. This is the conclusion that one reaches by examining Luther's *Lectures on Hebrews* primarily in the light of medieval exegesis of Hebrews. While the basic approach to Hebrews for medieval exegetes involved a judgment about the comparative excellence of the New Testament over the Old, for Luther it meant that discussion of the new was on a completely different level than the old. Discussion of the new meant Christ, who could not be compared with anyone or anything.

The medievals, including Augustine, considered the relationship between the two Testaments largely in hermeneutical and providential terms. The hermeneutical concerns were with questions of the various senses and their relationship, with promise/fulfillment, shadow/truth, and similar schemes. The providential categories were cast in terms of the divine plan of salvation and the processes of natural maturation. In short, the questions dealt with the two great eras covered by the two great Testaments.

Luther discusses the question largely in soteriological terms. In his Gloss he does repeat the various hermeneutical comparatives in the Epistle. And the problem of Pauline authorship discussed in the Gloss is raised because of the lack of relationship between the two Testaments in some texts—that is, questionable references in Hebrews to the Old Testament (Heb. 9, 4, 19-21; 12, 21). In contrast, medieval exegetes, with the exception of Erasmus, begin with the assumption that Paul

---

[165] *WA* 57. III. 192. 16-25.

[166] *WA* 57. III. 50. 16-17: "Arguit a minori probans Christi redemptionem esse aeternam, quia aliam quam veteram."

is the author and, therefore, his references to the Old Testament are
to be accepted. Furthermore, for them the New is a fuller revelation
of the Old. In his *Dictata*, Luther sees Paul in Hebrews as an hermeneutical guide to the Old Testament, which only intensifies Luther's
search for the harmony of Hebrews with the Old Testament. In his
Lectures on Hebrews there is then, some concern for hermeneutical
continuity between the two Testaments, but mostly the concern is
with the soteriological antitheses.[167]

His hermeneutical and soteriological interests are related in part,
in that, as is often said, if he were on a faculty today, he would be
labeled Professor of Old Testament Theology. Perhaps a reason why
Luther became so preoccupied with the Old Testament is that he felt
that the Old Testament is more Christological than the New.[168]

C. Young Luther

It remains here our task to gain a more complete understanding of
the theology of the young Luther on the problem of the relationship
between the two testaments. Ebeling recognizes the problem of the
two testaments in Luther's *Dictata*, but the discussion is brief and
is only in terms of law/gospel and the hermeneutical unity of Scripture.[169] Preus, concentrating as does Ebeling upon Luther's hermeneutic in the *Dictata*, has recently offered the development thesis that
Luther is "medieval" in his understanding of the Old Testament in
the earlier part of his *Dictata* (Pss. 1-84).[170] We will proceed here by

---

[167] We, then, have found the *Lectures on Hebrews* to be far more theological than
has Vogelsang.

[168] *WA* 3. 553. 24-26: "Vetus lex frequentius loquitur ad deum filium, sicut lex
nova ad patrem. Unde et ps. 101 Apostolus Hebr. 1 exponit tanquam ad Christum
dictus sit."

[169] Gerhard Ebeling, "Die Anfänge von Luthers Hermeneutik," *Zeitschrift für
Theologie und Kirche* 48 (1951), pp. 208, 211.

[170] James Samuel Preus, *From Shadow to Promise. Old Testament Interpretation
from Augustine to the Young Luther* (Cambridge, 1969), p. 155. The "medieval Luther"
for Preus is one who places the "hermeneutical divide" between the books of the Old
and New Testaments (*Ibid.*, p. 169). I have difficulty in accepting the thesis that Luther
in the early *Dictata* views the relationship between the two Testaments as one between
two distinct eras of salvation represented by the books of the two Testaments. Cf.
John Pilch, "Luther's Hermeneutical Shift," *Harvard Theological Review* 60 (1970),

examining the question of testament in its own right. In order to examine the development, if any, in Luther's theology of testament and to organize the material, we will concentrate mainly on those verses in the *Dictata* which Luther also deals with in his *Lectures on Hebrews* (and, where applicable, in his *Lectures on Romans*). Other material from the *Dictata* will be included when pertinent.

Ps. 18, 8 and Heb. 4, 12

An indication of the direction of Luther's theology of testament is given in his exegesis of Ps. 18, 8 in the *Dictata* and the *Lectures on Hebrews*. "The law of the Lord is spotless, converting souls" (Ps. 18, 8), which means it is not the law of Moses making demands on the "hand" (*Dictata*)[171] but it is the *Word* of the Lord, which is "living and active" (Heb. 4, 12), cleansing the "heart" (*Lectures on Hebrews*).[172]

In the *Dictata* on Ps. 1, 2, referring to Ps. 18, 8 and Heb. 4, 12, Luther identifies "law of the Lord" (Ps. 1, 2; 18, 8) with Word of the Lord (Heb. 4, 12), with the "gospel" and with the "law of Christ" which is only seized by faith.[173] Faith adhering to the Word purifies the heart and becomes, like the Word, *iustus* (Ps. 18, 8; Heb. 3, 12) both in Old Testament and New Testament.[174] The Word (law, gospel) is a message to the heart cleansed by faith.

Ps. 24 and Heb. 9

Another cluster of texts involving Ps. 24 and Heb. 9, give us an indication of the relation of the new testament to the old. In his *Dictata* on Ps. 24, 14, cited in the *Lectures on Hebrews* 9, 17, Luther

---

pp. 445-48. I also have difficulty with Preus' interpretation of the medievals, particularly Augustine, according to which the "divide" is between the books. I suspect the situation is far more complex.

[171] *WA* 3. 128. 17-18.

[172] *WA* 57. III. 161. 8-11.

[173] *WA* 55. II. 31. 4-32. 10.

[174] *WA* 57. III. 147. 20-148. 7: "Fides enim verbi purificat, quia sicut verbum Dei est purissimum et optimum, ita facit eum, qui adheret ei, similem sui purum et bonum, et omnino, quicquid ipsum habet et potest, impertit suo adherenti et credenti, psal. 18: 'Lex Domini immaculata convertens animas.' Et Christus Joan. 15.: 'Vos mundi estis propter sermonem, quem locutus sum vobis.' Ita et psal. 50. dicitur Hebraice: 'Tibi soli peccavi, propterea iustificabis in verbo tuo, mundabis in iudicando te.' Iste est iustus, sapiens, verus, bonus etc., qui credit in verbum Dei."

says that the mystery of the new testament (law, *pactum*) is manifest
only to those who fear the Lord.[175]

In his *Lectures on Hebrews* 9, 17, Luther refers to testament as the
promise which was contained in all the laws of Moses:

> The apostle here clearly lays open the allegorical interpretation of the law of Moses,
> whereby everything in the law was a promise and sign of Christ. Thus, as seen
> above, his death, the death of him who was to be true God and true man, had
> been decided upon in former times to be a testament and promise. For since God
> could not die, but at the same time had promised that he would die when he made
> this testament, it was necessary that he become man and fulfill that which he
> had promised.[176]

The Mosaic law, then, contains the promise and testament of Christ.
In the *Dictata* on Ps. 24, 10, cited in the *Lectures on Hebrews* 9, 24,
Luther says that all who seek the new testament which is spiritual, will
find that "All the ways of the Lord are mercy and truth" (Ps. 24, 10).[177]

In his commentary on Ps. 24, 12, Luther uses law and gospel inter-
changeably.[178] In the *Lectures on Hebrews* 9, 24, Luther asks, "How
were the saints of the Old Testament justified?" His answer, drawing
on Ps. 24, 10 and other texts, is that their obedience to the law was
rooted in faith and thus "their works of the law were at the same
time inwardly spiritual and outwardly corporeal, because 'for the
saints all things work together for their good' (Rom. 8, 28), and 'all
the ways of the righteous are mercy and truth' (Ps. 24, 10)."[179] The
new testament is contained and expressed in the old to him who sees
by faith both gospel and promise in the law.[180]

---

[175] *WA* 3. 144. 22-25.

[176] *WA* 57. III. 211. 16-22.

[177] *WA* 3. 144. 8-11.

[178] *WA* 3. 144. 15-17: " 'Quis est homo qui timet dominum,' q.d. non quero, quis
sit filius Israel: 'legem' Evangelium 'statuit' Dominus 'ei in via quam elegit' scilicet
Dominus, vel ipse timens Dominum." Cf. *WA* 3. 278. 7-10: " 'Congregate' vos angelice
virtutes 'illi sanctos eius' in se et aliis: 'qui ordinant' ordinate tradiderunt et disposu-
erunt 'testamentum eius' legem evangeliumque 'super sacrificia' ad sacrificandum
ei et colendum." 4. 42. 4: " 'Avertisti' avertere fecisti, ut non reciperent eam impii,
'testamentum' legem 'servi tui' Christi et populi eius." 4. 44. 7-9: " 'Avertisti' scilicet
ab illis ad gentes 'testamentum' evangelium 'servi tui,' ut Matt. 21 'auferetur a vobis
regnum.' "

[179] *WA* 57. III. 216. 20-217. 1; 217. 21-22.

[180] *WA* 3. 157. 28-34.

Ps. 32, 6-9 and Heb. 1, 8

Even on the basis of the texts cited thus far, it is becoming clear that for the young Luther the relationship between the old and new testaments is not one between two distinct eras of salvation, represented by the books of the two Testaments, but it is between two ways of receiving the one testament, Word, promise, gospel.

In both the *Dictata* on Ps. 32, 6-7 and the *Lectures on Hebrews* 1, 8, citing Ps. 32, 6f., the *verbum, gratia, evangelium, virga*, remain constant from generation to generation. In the *Dictata* Luther says that the Church "conveys" (*transfundit*) the Word from people to people. There are two kinds of vessels: old and new, that is, "people of the old and new testament." The people are plural, divided into flesh and spirit, but the testament is singular.[181]

In the *Lectures on Hebrews* Luther says that Christ has ruled his kingdom from the beginning only by the one *virga*: "the gospel or the Word of God."[182] Luther then, draws a parallel between the old and new testament and the old and new vessel, the flesh and spirit.

Ps. 44, 3 and Heb. 8, 10

Ps. 44, 3, cited in the *Lectures on Romans, Galatians* and *Hebrews*, leads further into the twofold character of the singular testament. In the *Dictata* on this verse ("Grace is poured upon your lips") Luther lists various senses of the *labia Christi*. He says they are "both testaments spiritually heard and presented."[183] Both testaments have the same character, i.e., they need to be spiritually understood through grace in order to be properly understood. The Word of the new law, identified with the gospel and the spirit of the old law, is always poured out through grace (Is. 55, 11). In the *Lectures on Romans*, Luther understands Ps. 44, 3 to mean that, inasmuch as the law promises and the gospel sets forth (*exhibet*) Christ, the proper reception of Christ is to receive the gospel from the law and the gospel from

---

181 *WA* 3. 184. 25-30: "Sic Ecclesia a generatione in generationem transfundit vinum et oleum suum, verbum et gratiam Dei. Sunt autem utres veteres et novi, id est populi novi et veteris testamenti. Et 'vinum novum non in utres veteres.' Sic ait dominus, quando voluit facere distinctionem inter consolationem carnis et spiritus. Quia homo carnalis non capit consolationem spiritus."

182 *WA* 57. III. 108. 15-109. 2.

183 *WA* 3. 259. 1-3.

the gospel, i.e., to receive Christ from the word of grace.[184] The point of Ps. 44, 3 in the *Lectures on Galatians* is that the gospel announces grace, not knowledge.[185] In his *Lectures on Hebrews* 8, 10, Luther says that the Word of the new testament proclaims that which is of the spirit by the Word of grace according to Ps. 44, 3.[186] This set of texts indicates that the Word, without reference to time, can be received as letter, old testament, or as spirit, new testament, and it all depends on the "pouring out" of grace.

Ps. 67, 14 and Heb. 6, 12

Up until now one of the main thrusts of the texts has been that testament as Word of the Lord is singular and that the distinction, old and new testament, refers to the type of response by man. Now we can go further into the relationship between the old and new testaments. In his *Dictata* on Ps. 67, 14, cited in the *Lectures on Hebrews* 6, 12, Luther identifies "lots" (*cleros, sortes*) as "two testaments." Thus the sense of the verse ("If you sleep in the midst of lots") in the *Dictata* is that a man of faith lives between the two testaments, i.e., between the temporal and the celestial.[187]

Luther uses this verse in his *Lectures on Hebrews* to draw a parallel between the Christian and Christ on the cross. As Christ on the cross was suspended in the air between heaven and earth, "thus the faithful are suspended between heaven and earth, and 'sleep' as the psalm says, 'in the midst of lots,' that is, they are crucified with Christ lifted in the air."[188] The two testaments coexist as the man of faith lives in an "in between" (*inter medias*) situation. The coexistence is permanent because the man of faith always lives between the testaments.

In his *Dictata* on Ps. 90, 4, Luther interprets the phrase: "Under his wings you will hope (*sperabis*)," to mean: "Under the two testaments you will be nourished through hope."[189] The two wings are "the two

---

[184] *WA* 56. 338. 14-26.

[185] *WA* 57. II. 60. 20-22.

[186] *WA* 57. III. 195. 22-24: "Novi testamenti haec est gratia, quod verbum et litterae eius docent ea, quae spiritus sunt, et verba gratiae dicuntur iuxta illud psalmi 44: 'Diffusa est gratia in labiis tuis.' "

[187] *WA* 3. 386. 15-17: " 'Si dormiatis' a tumultu cupiditatum quiescentes 'inter medios cleros' duo testamenta, vel fide inter temporalia et celestia vivere." Cf. 396. 9 ff.

[188] *WA* 57. III. 185. 2-8.

[189] *WA* 4. 68. 20-21.

testaments" (*sinistra* and *dextera*).[190] God protects the faithful[191] with both testaments, under both the left and right wings.

The two testaments can refer to different things, temporal/eternal, two aspects of God's protection, dialectical response (*inter medias*) of the same person, two antithetical responses (flesh, spirit) of different people. Most often the two testaments are the two possibilities of hearing or not hearing.

Ps. 103, 3, 10 and Heb. 1, 7

In his *Dictata* on Ps. 103, 3, cited in the *Lectures on Hebrews* 1, 7, Luther clearly relates the old and new testaments with the old and new law and with the old and new man. In his fourfold exegesis of the verse ("Who walkest upon the wings of the winds") the allegorical meaning of wings (*due penne*) is "the two testaments." Luther's point is that the old and new "unite" (*iunguntur, conveniunt*) as the old is killed and the new born. The old brings death, and new life. Each testament is seen for what it is only in relation to the other. Every *doctor* should have both possible testaments in focus to teach—to destroy the old and build the new—so that he does not put new wine in old wineskins.[192]

In the context of the same psalm, verse 10 ("Thou sendest forth springs in the valleys"), Luther says that "the old and new law make the same valley," like two mountains having the same valley. The two "come together in one Church, in one Spirit, in one base (*radice*) of truth, in one faith, in one humility, although in their peaks (*vertice*) they differ." The Church in this life exists in the midst of the two mountains, "that is, between the old and new law which unite harmoniously. 'If you sleep in the midst of lots,' and so on. These are

---

190 *WA* 4. 68. 34 and footnote.

191 *WA* 4. 62. 1.

192 *WA* 4. 176. 26-36: "Tercio Penne due sunt duo testamenta, Ventorum, id est spirituarium hominum, doctorum, prelatorum. Et iste due penne singulorum iunguntur, quia vetus et nova lex conveniunt, sicut homo vetus occisus et homo novus suscitatus. Vetus lex hominem veterem monstrat mortuum, nova vivum novum exhibet. Et sic amice conveniunt, ut supra dictum. Unde et Angeli pinguntur et finguntur duabus alis et Cherubin similiter. Quia omnis doctor duo testamenta debet habere, sicut dominus Matth. 13. docuit dicens: 'omnis scriba doctus in regno coelorum similis est homini patrifamilias, qui profert de thezauro suo nova et vetera.' Quia de homine novo et vetere debet loqui et docere, quomodo ille destruatur et iste edificetur, ne vinum novum in utres veteres immittat, sed in novos etc."

the two testaments, the two lots, two heritages by which the Church is instructed in this life" (Ps. 67, 14).[193] The two testaments then, remain separate (*vertice*) but also together (*radice*) in this life. At the base (*radice*) of experience then, the two testaments involve each other.

It might be more accurate to speak of Luther's theology of testament (in the singular). The *testamentum dei* (singular) equals *promissio Christi*. In his *Dictata* on Ps. 77, 10, Luther identifies "testamentum dei" as "the law which testifies to future grace in faith or to the law of Christ."[194] Law equals testament. Testament is constant. In his *Lectures on Galatians* 3, 17, Luther draws on Ps. 80, 9 and Heb. 9, 17 to show that in Scripture promise, testament, *pactum* all refer to *passio Dei*—all refer to the death of the God-man which confirms or validates the testament.[195] The *testamentum Christi* is the promise or testament of God (law as well as gospel) that the death of Christ

---

[193] *WA* 4. 179. 30-180. 9: "Sed notandum singulariter, quod 'in convallibus' dicit, quia mons et mons habent eandem vallem. Sic vetus lex et nova lex faciunt eandem vallem. Et ideo dicitur 'Convallis' propter consortium lateralis montis, ut si mons monti dicat: 'Vallis mea est tue convallis, et vallis tua mee convallis, quia eandem vallem habemus et communi valle concordamus.' Et hee convalles sunt diverse Ecclesie singulatim. Nam et multi sunt montes hinc et inde, multi Apostoli et multi prophete, quorum quilibet duo faciunt convallem suam, immo omnes convalles. Secundo notandum, quod convalles in radicibus sunt montium, non in cacumine. Quia scilicet prophete et Evangelium conveniunt in una Ecclesia, in uno spiritu, in una radice veritatis, in una fide, in una humilitate, licet in vertice differant. Quia illa in gloria seculi, ista in gloria coeli altissima est. Et illa velut pars seu collis inferior, ista autem superior. Unde et illa ps. 41 dicitur 'Mons modicus,' nostra autem 'mons magnus et superior,' sive 'mons excelsus' Matth. 17. Sic ergo Ecclesia intra medium duorum montium versatur in hac vita, id est inter veterem et novam legem concordantes. Ps. 67. 'Si dormiatis inter medios cleros etc.' Hec sunt duo testamenta, due sortes, due hereditates, quibus instruitur Ecclesia in hac vita."

[194] *WA* 3. 552. 5-6.

[195] *WA* 57. II. 82. 2-15: "Quia Apostolus promissiones Dei vocat 'testamentum,' sicut et alibi in Scripturis vocatur, ut psal. 81: 'Audi, Israhel, et contestabor tibi' etc., manifeste indicat futurum fuisse, ut Deus aliquando moreretur et sic in promissione Dei tanquam in nuncupato testamento suo incarnatio simul et passio Dei intelligeretur. Quia, ut Hebre. 9., 'testamentum in mortuis confirmatur.' Quare nec Dei testamentum confirmari potuit, nisi Deus ipse testator moreretur. Unde ibidem nono de Christo 'Idcirco novi testamenti mediator est, ut morte intercedente repromissionem accipiant.' Hinc etiam concordatur ista differentia, quod beatus Ieronimus 'pactum' pocius quam 'testamentum' dicendum putat. Nam qui paciscitur, vivus manet, qui testatur, moriturus est; ita Ihesus Christus ut Deus immortalis fecit pactum, idem simul et testamentum, quia futurus mortalis, quare recte idem est pactum et testamentum, sicut idem Christus est Deus et homo."

is to demonstrate (*exhibitio*) the faithfulness of God. Luther's *theologia crucis* is a *theologia testamenti*.

D. Conclusion

The purpose of this chapter has been to see what light Augustine and medieval exegesis of Hebrews shed on Luther's *Lectures on Hebrews*. treating the two testaments in soteriological terms. It has been the study of Augustine that has opened up to us various possible approaches to the question of the relationship between the two Testaments.[196] By taking only a hermeneutical approach, such as Ebeling, Preus, and others, one comes up with hermeneutical conclusions. By raising providential and soteriological questions, such as does Augustine, one sees other possibilities.

The study of Luther and Augustine seems to be emerging again as a critical area of Luther research. All I can conclude at this point on the question of the two Testaments is that both Augustine and Luther treat the question in soteriological terms; Luther perhaps more so. In fact, the theology of the young Luther might well be called a theology of testament, that is, the category of *testamentum* seems to account for more of the pieces than, for example, *theologia crucis, doctor fidei, promissio*. Of course any such labeling is reductionistic, but approaching such a heresy on the historiographical horizon is not all bad. As to the content of the soteriology of Augustine and Luther, I can only suggest the following, approached from the category of *testamentum*: Augustine reads *testamentum, pactum, placitum*, as *pactum inter*. His sanative metaphor of *pactum medicinae* and the conditions for membership in a testament described as "belonging," "tasting," "desiring," also suggest that *testamentum* is a bilateral and developmental concept for Augustine. Luther reads *testamentum, pactum, promissio* as a unilateral and dialectical testament. A more complete understanding of Augustine then, has allowed us to approach the question of the relationship between the two Testaments in more than hermeneutical terms. Over against the medieval exegetical tradition, the argument of this chapter has been that the fundamental force

---

[196] We have found Augustine's and Luther's theology of God and man to be far more complex than does Hamel.

of Luther's interpretation comes into focus, and it is the absolute
antithesis between the two testaments as two ways of salvation. In
the light of Luther's earlier exegetical work, we have seen that his
more complete understanding of the two testaments is that their
relationship is not only antithetical but also dialectical. For Luther
in his *Dictata* there do seem to be men who during the time of the
Old Testament "until today" have received the *testamentum dei* only
as letter.[197] Luther's *theologia crucis* in his *Lectures on Hebrews* is that
revelation comes under opposites.[198] To see the new is to see the old as
old. To accept the new is to reject the old—a constant struggle.[199]
The cross reveals that we are sinners and yet justified. As Christ is
lifted between earth and heaven the Christian exists between the two
testaments. The contrast is a continuous struggle within each and
every man. In a phrase, we might suggest the relationship for Luther
is *simul vetus et novum testamentum*.

For the young Luther then, up to 1517-18, only one Word comes
forth from God. That word is constant and the same. It is variously
called testament, promise, law, gospel. In this context the designation
of old and new testament does not refer to two different testaments
of God; rather during the time covered by the books of both the Old
and New Testaments, the one testament of God is the *testamentum
Christi*. The testament of God becomes old when it is received by man
as law; just as it becomes new when it is received by man as spirit.
The difference between old and new testament is with man, not with
God. The two testaments refer to two different types of men and
two different responses in one and the same man. There are old
testament men and new testament men and every man of faith is
radically caught (*radice*) between the testaments (*vertice*), during the
time covered by the books of the Old and New Testaments. The
difference between the testaments is the difference between receiving
the *testamentum dei et Christi* as letter or spirit, as old or new. With
reference to God there is one testament; with reference to men there
are two.

For the young Luther the relationship between the two testaments
is not primarily a hermeneutical question of the relation of the books
of the Old and New Testament, that is, a "senses" question. Nor is

---

[197] *WA* 3. 145. 27.
[198] *WA* 57. III. 79. 16-80. 11.
[199] *WA* 3. 290. 4-13.

it a providential question. For him it is a question of hearing the Word of testament or covenant in any period of time, that is, it is a soteriological question of covenant as testament. The soteriological possibilities described in the books are antithetical and dialectical: *simul vetus et novum testamentum.*

CHAPTER THREE

THE CONCEPT OF FAITH

Luther's theology of testament came into focus through a comparison with medieval exegetes of Hebrews, and St. Augustine. In the *Lectures on Hebrews* Luther emphasizes the soteriological antithesis between the two testaments over against medieval exegetes who develop in various ways the hermeneutical and providential theme of *excellentia Christi* in comparison with the Old Testament. In the light of Luther's earlier exegesis it became apparent that the difference and contrast between the two testaments for him is faith—the two testaments represent two types of response to the Word.

The concern of this chapter and the next will be to develop two integral aspects of Luther's theology of testament. The antithetical and dialectical character of the relationship between the two testaments is the struggle of faith. Several of the secondary studies cite the concept of faith and Christology as key themes in Luther's *Lectures on Hebrews*. None gives an analysis of Luther in relation to previous exegesis. Since Luther's understanding of the relationship between the two testaments came into focus by a comparison with medieval exegesis, we will now see what light it sheds on Luther's theology of faith.[1]

Luther's discussion of faith in the *Lectures on Hebrews* entails four basic elements, it seems to me. Faith comes from hearing the Word, cleanses the heart, possesses things hoped for and is the certitude of salvation. In the light of medieval exegesis the first aspect of his understanding of faith, hearing the Word of faith, can be seen in his interpretation of Hebrews 3, 5 and 3, 7; the second, faith cleanses the heart, in Hebrews 3, 12-13 and 9, 14; the third, faith possesses things hoped for, in Hebrews 3, 14 and 11, 1; and the fourth, faith is the personal certitude of salvation, in Hebrews 5, 1 and 9, 24.

---

[1] Just as it is impossible for this study to include a comparison of Luther and Augustine on soteriology, so also a comparison of the two on faith and Christology would require a separate study.

A. Hearing the Word of Faith

3,5. "Now Moses was faithful in all God's house as a servant, for a witness of those things that were to be spoken later."

Luther directs his attention to the statement that Moses was a "witness." It immediately becomes clear that Moses as "witness" means for Luther preacher of God's Word: "God refers to his Word and his preachers in our text as 'witnesses.' "[2] This interpretation of Luther's is striking in the light of medieval exegesis.

Chrysostom sets the stage for medieval exegesis of 3, 5 by discussing the verse under the rubric of the comparative "excellentia" of Christ in comparison to Moses.[3] The *Glossa interlinearis* says that Moses as "witness" testified to that which was appropriate "for carnal men not yet capable of understanding spiritual matters."[4] The *Glossa ordinaria* emphasizes the difference between Christ as builder of his own house and Moses as occupant of another's house and between Christ as Son and Moses as servant. The *Glossa ordinaria* says that Moses handed down "carnal matters to carnal men," whereas Christ bequeathed spiritual matters.[5] Aquinas and Tarantasia likewise emphasize the superiority of Christ over Moses. The superiority is proven, they argue, in the comparison between Moses as servant in his lord's house and Christ as Son in his own house.[6] Tarantasia claims that "those things that were to be said" applied to "that time" and to "the carnal Jews."

Luther, in contrast to these medieval exegetes, interprets both the "witness" of Moses and the witness of Christ to be a testimony of God's Word, a testimony of the gospel. Moses' message was a "testimonium" and "the Word of God is most appropriately called a 'testimonium.' "[7] Luther, then, does not discuss the relative excellence of Christ. Nor does he regard Moses' "witness" as carnal. Rather, Moses' "testimonium" is the Word of God, the gospel, not the law.

Though Moses and Christ are similarly described here as "witnesses" of the gospel, this does not mean for Luther that the two Testaments

---

[2] *WA* 57. III. 138. 1920.
[3] Chrysostom, p. 274.
[4] *Glossa interlinearis*, f. 139r.
[5] *Glossa ordinaria*, f. 139r.
[6] Aquinas, p. 373; Tarantasia, p. 180.
[7] *WA* 57. III. 139. 13.

nor that Moses and Christ are comparable. It is their "witness" of the gospel that is comparable.

The importance of Moses' *testimonium* or any *testimonium* of God's Word, according to Luther, is that it is a "Word of faith," a witness about the future, received only by hearing. In his *Dictata* on Ps. 80, 9, cited in the *Lectures on Hebrews* 3, 5, Luther says that the witness is a "law of faith, a witness of future realities and evidence of things not seen."[8] On Heb. 3, 5 Luther says:

> God refers to his Word and his preachers in our text as "witnesses," as, for example, in Ps. 81, 8: "Hear, O my people, and I will witness to you." The Latin language cannot sufficiently explain this verb "to witness" in one word. But the meaning is this: in the future, I will speak a Word in the midst of you or among you. For the Hebrew has: "I will witness unto you." This Word will not reveal things of the present, but will be a witness of things not seen. Therefore, it is essential that you hear what you cannot see or grasp.[9]

The characteristic of a *testimonium* is that it is *audibile*. It can only be grasped by the ear, that is, by faith:

> For what Christ has said about heaven and the future life will only be grasped by hearing, since it not only surpasses all our understanding, be it ever so deep, but also all our desires, be they ever so wide. Therefore, the witness of the Lord is a Word of faith and a hidden wisdom, understood by children. Isaiah too describes it as received by the ear (53, 1): "Lord, who has believed what we have heard?" that is, who has heard our voice when we preach the gospel.
> The Word of God is most appropriately called a "witness." For just as in legal disputes, where one makes a judgment on the reports of witnesses from only hearing them and believing them, because there is no other way, not even by perception or reason, so also the gospel is received in no other way than by hearing.[10]

3,7. "Therefore as the Holy Spirit says: 'Today if you hear his voice, do not harden your hearts.'"

Luther continues his discussion of faith as hearing in his exegesis of 3, 7. He makes it clear that the "hearing" of faith is specifically the "hearing" of the *verbum Dei*, which is a striking claim in the light of medieval exegesis. Also striking is Luther's conclusion that "it is the worst thing possible to throw oneself into doing works before God works in us, that is, before we believe."[11]

The importance of this conclusion is brought to light by a comparison

---

[8] *WA* 3. 611. 16-19.
[9] *WA* 57. III. 138. 19-139. 2.
[10] *WA* 57. III. 139. 4-16.
[11] *WA* 57. III. 143. 5-6.

of Luther's summary of the themes preceding and following 3, 7 and
the summaries of his medieval predecessors. In his Gloss on the word
"therefore," Luther says, "After Paul has praised Christ the Apostle
and his glory, he now begins to urge us to have faith in him."[12] The
Glossa ordinaria, Aquinas, Tarantasia, Lyra and Dionysius the Carthusian describe the theme preceding 3, 7 as the *excellentia Christi*
compared with the angels, prophets and Moses, which leads them to
the conclusion that since Christ is greater than these he ought to be
diligently obeyed.[13] Tarantasia says that Christ ought to be diligently
heard. Medieval exegetes emphasize the doing of obedience, whereas
Luther emphasizes the hearing of faith and perhaps regarded this
medieval emphasis on obedience to be an emphasis on "doing works
before God works in us":

> It should be noted that this is the greatest single thing which God requires of
> the Jews, indeed of all men, namely, that they hear his voice. Thus Moses empha-
> sizes throughout Deuteronomy: "Hear, O Israel," and: "If you hear the voice
> of the Lord, your God." So much so that Jeremiah says (7, 21-23): "Add your
> burnt offerings to your sacrifices, and eat the flesh. For in the day that I brought
> them out of the land of Egypt, I did not speak to your fathers or command them
> concerning burnt offerings and sacrifices. But this command I gave them, saying:
> 'Hear my voice, and I will be your God, and you shall be my people.' " Indeed
> nothing resounds in the prophets more frequently than the words "hear," "listen
> you," "they did not hear" and "they were unwilling to hear." And rightly so,
> because it is impossible for God to be with us effectively if faith is absent, since
> he does everything through his Word alone. Thus no one is able to cooperate with
> him unless he adheres to the Word through faith, just as an instrument does not
> cooperate with the artist unless it is taken in his hand. Therefore, it is the worst
> thing possible to throw oneself into doing works before God works in us, that is,
> before we believe.[14]

That which faith hears, according to Luther, is the *verbum Dei*,
the voice of Christ speaking directly to the hearer:

> "When you hear his voice," is a typically Hebrew phrase. It is a statement of
> fact rather than a conditional phrase. Thus it means: "After you have become
> hearers," or: "After you have heard his voice," that is, heard by his voice, "for
> hearing comes by the Word of Christ" (Rom. 10, 17). The Hebrew text carries
> a more profound meaning than our Vulgate translation. The Hebrew expresses

---

[12] *WA* 57. III. 17. 15-22.

[13] *Glossa ordinaria*, f. 139r; Aquinas, pp. 374-75; Tarantasia, p. 181; Lyra, f. 139r;
Dionysius the Carthusian, p. 483.

[14] *WA* 57. III. 142. 18-143. 6.

the promise that [God] will open our ears through the voice of Christ, which is
to say: when he himself speaks and makes you hear, you will not harden your
hearts.[15]

Medieval exegetes hold that one hears Christ in the gospel, namely,
the historical teaching of Jesus Christ and the Apostles. The *Glossa
ordinaria*, Aquinas, Tarantasia, and Lyra discuss the different ways
God spoke in the two Testaments. In the Old Testament God spoke
through Moses, the prophets and the angels. In the New Testament
God spoke through Christ.[16] "The gospel is the voice of Christ," says
Tarantasia. He and Lyra cite Matt. 5, 2, "And he opened his mouth
and taught them." Burgos discusses the claim that if Israel were to
repent for one day the Messiah would come immediately. If they
would listen to the voice of God he would come immediately, "for
they who hear his voice, namely the voice of Christ through faith,
he comes to them immediately."[17]

For Luther the upshot of 3, 7 is the necessity for man to hear the
verbum Dei. In his *Dictata* on Ps. 31, 9, cited in the *Lectures on Hebrews*
3, 7, Luther says that "the horse and the mule"—*carnales*—follow
only the "*sensibilia*" and not the "*invisibilia et spiritualia*."[18] In the
Lectures on Hebrews Luther says that those who do not hear the
verbum Dei

> are like the horse and the mule who obey their master as long as they have some-
> thing to go by, but when this is no longer the case, they run off. Therefore, faith
> in Christ is the hardest thing one can imagine, because one is caught up and taken
> up from everything which one experiences within and without to the things which
> one senses neither within nor without, namely, to the invisible, most high and
> incomprehensible God.[19]

With reference to 10, 5, Luther says that hearing the *verbum Dei* is
what makes a man worthy of the name Christian. The sole and
necessary "organ" of the Christian is his ears:

> There is no extraordinary force and power in the word "ears." In the new law
> all the infinite burdens of ceremonies, that is, occasions for sin, have been taken
> away. Nor does God require feet or hands or any other member, except ears, so
> that all burdens have been reduced to one simple way of life. If you were to ask
> a Christian what his task is and by what he is worthy of the name Christian, there

---

15 *WA* 57. III. 142. 10-16.
16 *Glossa ordinaria*, f. 139r-139v; Tarantasia, p. 181; Lyra, f. 139r.
17 Burgos, f. 140r.
18 *WA* 3. 173. 33-36.
19 *WA* 57. III. 44. 5-12.

could be no other response than hearing the Word of God, that is, faith. Ears are the only organs of the Christian man, because he is justified by faith and judged a Christian not by any works of his members.[20]

B. Cleansing of the Heart

3,12-13. "Take care, brethren, lest there be in any of you an evil heart, leading you to fall away from the living God. [v. 13.] But exhort one another every day, as long as it is called 'today,' that none of you may be hardened by the deceitfulness of sin."

Luther holds that the key to 3, 12 is the word "heart." He interprets the verse as an exhortation for one to be sure that his heart is "clean." Faith cleanses the heart. Through faith united to Christ who is the *verbum Dei* man becomes "clean," "pure," "just," "wise," "good" and so on:

> The whole emphasis of this text is on the word "heart." For he does not say: Take care lest there be in any of you a greedy hand, a deceitful eye or a lustful ear. One ought above all to take care that his heart is good, pure, and holy, as in Ps. 51, 10: "Create in me a clean heart, O God, and renew a right spirit within me." This implies that any purity in the works of the body is nothing unless there first be purity of the heart.... Therefore the heart only becomes pure and good through faith in Christ, as in Acts 15, 9: "He purified their hearts by faith, making no distinction between us and them." Faith in the Word purifies, because, just as the Word of God is completely pure and good, so he who adheres to it becomes like the Word, pure and good. In general, whatever the Word possesses and is able to give, it shares with him who adheres to it and believes it.... He who believes in the Word of God is just, wise, true, good, and so on.[21]

Luther is concerned to differentiate between the "heart" and the "hand," that is, between faith and works. Purity of the heart is the chief concern of the Christian, a claim which stands out in the light of medieval exegesis. Aquinas, Tarantasia and Lyra exegete the verse as an exhortation to do good works.[22]

The same contrast between Luther's interpretation and that of medieval exegetes is again prominent in the context of 3, 13. Some medieval exegetes interpret the verse as an admonition for the increase of virtue (the *Glossa interlinearis*), the doing of good (Aquinas), and

---

[20] *WA* 57. III. 222. 1-9.

[21] *WA* 57. III. 147. 10-148. 7.

[22] Aquinas, p. 377; Tarantasia, p. 183; Lyra, f. 139v.

the zeal for progress (Tarantasia).[23] Luther contends that the exhortation of 3, 13 is for the "mediating," "reading," and "listening" to the *verbum Dei*: "Just as man's body becomes weak without its daily bread, so also his heart cannot become strong without the bread of God's Word."[24] For Luther the "deceitfulness of sin" is the love of one's own virtue and righteousness—faith is the sum and substance of all virtue:

> As a corollary it follows that faith in Christ is all virtue and unfaith all vice, as sufficiently explained above. It is through faith that man becomes like the Word of God. This Word now is the Son of God. Thus everyone who believes in him is a son of God (John 1, 12), without any sin and full of all virtue. On the other hand, every unbeliever is full of all vice and evil. He is, namely, a son of the devil and iniquity.[25]

9,14. "How much more shall the blood of Christ, who through the Holy Spirit offered himself without blemish to God, cleanse our conscience from dead works to serve the living God?"

The main theme of Luther's exegesis of this verse is the purity of conscience through faith. From the perspective of different segments of the exegetical tradition different aspects of this theme and its meaning for Luther stand out.

The first striking aspect of Luther's exegesis is his concern with the conscience. Medieval exegetes, interested generally in a comparison between the two Testaments, are interested here in a comparison between the cleansing of the blood of goats and bulls (v. 13) and the cleansing of Christ's blood. More specifically, Chrysostom and Alcuin concentrate on the nature of "dead works," their pollution, odor, corruption and similarity to a plague.[26] The only comment on "conscience" in the *Glossa interlinearis*, repeated by Tarantasia, reads "not the flesh only."[27] Aquinas and Lyra discuss the consequence of Christ's offering, saying that it is efficacious because of the fact that Christ made the offering, that it was made through the Holy Spirit out of love for God and the neighbor and that it was an immaculate offering.[28] Dionysius the Carthusian says that the conscience

---

[23] *Glossa interlinearis*, f. 139v.; Aquinas, p. 377; Tarantasia, p. 183.

[24] *WA* 57. III. 148. 19-149. 11.

[25] *WA* 57. III. 151. 13-18.

[26] Chrysostom, p. 338; Alcuin, p. 1073.

[27] Tarantasia, p. 229.

[28] Aquinas, p. 434; Lyra, f. 150v.

is cleansed "in baptism, or penance or the other sacraments, through which the virtue and merit of Christ is applied to us."[29] Faber Stapulensis, extensively contrasting the sacrifice of calves and bulls with the sacrifice of Christ, says that the former was carnal, the latter was spiritual, "superior" and "potentior," with the result that the latter "totally and spiritually purifies the conscience from all sin and adds justification and complete grace."[30]

Luther, in contrast to his predecessors, is interested in the conscience and the effect of sin on it, contrasted by the effect of faith. For Luther the conscience is the seat of memory and such emotions as fear, anxiety, dread and oppression on the one hand, and joy and peace on the other. The effect of sin on the conscience is the continual harassment of its memory and the anxiety, dread and fear of future retribution. The effect on the conscience of faith in the blood of Christ is the freedom from all such anxieties and the peace and joy in the forgiveness of sins:

> First of all, purity of conscience means that man is not attacked by the memory of his sins nor disquieted by the fear of future punishment, as Ps. 112, 7 says: "The righteous will not be afraid of evil tidings." Thus the evil conscience is caught and oppressed between past sin and future punishment. They are both causes of deep anxiety, as the prophet says. Thus Rom. 2, 9: "There will be tribulation and anxiety for every human being who does evil." Since there is no way to change past sin or avoid future wrath, the definite result is that whatever way the conscience turns it is anxious and oppressed. Only through the blood of Christ is it freed from these anxieties. If it relies on the blood of Christ in faith, it believes and knows that its sins have been washed and carried away in the blood. Thus the conscience is at the same time purified and given peace through faith, so that it no longer dreads punishment, because of joy in the forgiveness of sins.[31]

The second striking aspect of Luther's exegesis is his emphasis that the purity of conscience comes through faith. With the exception of Aquinas, faith is not mentioned by medieval exegetes in their interpretation of 9, 14. They all discuss the verse in terms of the historical work of Christ. In this light it is striking that Luther claims that Christ's blood by itself does not cleanse the conscience unless one believes in the forgiveness of sins:

> No law, no work, in fact nothing at all can effect this purity, except the blood of Christ alone, and not even Christ's blood unless a man in his heart believes

---

[29] Dionysius the Carthusian, pp. 506-507.
[30] Faber Stapulensis, f. 248v.
[31] *WA* 57. III. 207. 15-26.

that it was poured out for the forgiveness of sins. Thus one must believe him who made the testament. "This is my blood which is poured out for you and for many for the forgiveness of sins" (Matt. 26, 28).[32]

Luther's exegesis of 9, 14 is striking, finally, in the light of Aquinas' claim that the cleansing of the conscience "happens through faith—Acts 15, 9, 'cleansing their hearts through faith'—namely, faith which believes that all who adhere to Christ are cleansed through his blood."[33] Luther argues that objective faith is insufficient for the cleansing of the conscience. Aquinas's description of faith in Luther's language would be faith that "believes that the blood of Christ was poured out for the forgiveness of sins." This is objective faith in the work of Christ which does not necessarily entail personal faith in the forgiveness of one's very own sins, the only kind of faith for Luther sufficient for the forgiveness of sins:

> Therefore, it follows that a good, clean, peaceful and joyful conscience is the same as faith in the forgiveness of sins, which can only come about when faith is placed in that Word of God which proclaims that the blood of Christ was poured out for us for the forgiveness of sins. However much we see and hear that the blood of Christ was poured out, the conscience will not be cleansed by this unless the words, "for the forgiveness of sins," are added. For the Jews saw and the Gentiles heard, but they were not cleansed. In fact it is not sufficient to believe that the blood of Christ was poured out for the forgiveness of sins, unless one believes that it was poured out for the forgiveness of his own sins. Thus only through the pouring out of the blood of Christ is the conscience cleansed through faith in the Word of Christ.[34]

C. Possession of Things hoped for

3,14. "For we become partakers of Christ, if only we hold the beginning of his substance firm to the end."

In the context of 3, 14 and 11, 1 ("Faith is the substance of things hoped for") Luther distinguishes himself from his predecessors on the definition of "substance," and thereby deviates from the dominant understanding of faith in medieval exegesis of Hebrews. In the medieval exegetical tradition faith as "substance" is usually defined as the "foundation," "beginning," or "cause" of salvation. As foundation,

---

[32] *WA* 57. III. 207. 26-208. 4.
[33] Aquinas, p. 434.
[34] *WA* 57. III. 208. 22-209. 3.

faith is insufficient for salvation. It needs to be "built up" by works of love. Faith is only the first step in the process of sanctification, the first of a triad of theological virtues: faith, hope, love. Man is never "clean" and "just" in the present, but only perhaps, at the end of his life.

Chrysostom defines "substance" as "underlying reality" (*subsistentia*) or "essence" (*essentia*). " 'The beginning of substance' denotes faith, through which we are born, through which we exist and, so to say, through which we become true beings."[35] Chrysostom discusses his concept of faith further in the context of 6, 1. He holds that faith is the foundation (*initium* and *fundamentum*) for building a Christian life. By definition, "the beginning" means "there is not a virtuous life." Just as a building is more than a foundation, so faith needs to be "built upon" with an *optima* and *recta* life. The Christian life which Chrysostom calls for is one marked by "cleanliness."[36]

With reference to 3, 14, the *Glossa ordinaria* defines the "beginning of substance" as faith which is the "beginning of good." Faith is the beginning of God's dwelling in us and our salvation.[37]

Aquinas interprets faith as the basis of virtue and works of love. The "beginning of substance" is the "foundation" of "faith formed by works of love."[38] Faith along with fear as its "companion" is the basis of the spiritual virtues: faith, hope and love.[39] Elsewhere, he says that faith is the "origin of hope"[40] and the "foundation of the virtues."[41] In his discussion of 10, 22 and 10, 38 Aquinas makes it clear that faith alone is not sufficient for salvation. A "full faith" is required, that is, faith in the content of Christian teaching (*fides quae*) and faith formed by works of love (*fides formata*).[42] Faith without works of love is "dead."[43]

Tarantasia interprets faith as "substance" to mean the "beginning" and "foundation" of "all good" and "all virtue." The foundation of

---

[35] Chrysostom, p. 279.
[36] *Ibid.*, p. 299.
[37] *Glossa ordinaria*, f. 139v.
[38] Aquinas, p. 378.
[39] *Ibid.*, p. 379.
[40] *Ibid.*, p. 387.
[41] *Ibid.*, p. 398.
[42] *Ibid.*, p. 447.
[43] *Ibid.*, p. 454.

virtue, faith, was first laid by Christ. Virtue is Christ's "possession" and faith is the beginning of one's laying hold on this possession:

"In the beginning of his substance" is faith which is the beginning and foundation of the substance of Christ, that is, of all good and virtue. These are called the substance of Christ just as a possession is called the substance of the possessor. For Christ is the lord of virtue. Faith is the foundation of this possession and substance, because "No other foundation can anyone lay than that which is laid, which is Christ Jesus." (I Cor. 3, 11).[44]

Lyra and Dionysius the Carthusian interpret the conditional phrase, "if only we hold the beginning of his substance firm to the end," to mean that one joined to Christ in baptism must persevere in his "formed faith." The "beginning of his substance" means faith initially formed by works of love.[45] Faber Stapulensis says that the "beginning of substance" is the beginning of faith because "substance" refers to faith in 11, 1.[46]

Luther argues that "substance" in Heb. 3, 14 and particularly in 11, 1, as well as throughout Scripture, means "possession." In 3, 14 "substance" can be taken both as essence, as Chrysostom would have it, and as possession:

Here, therefore, "substance" means the supply or possession of goods. This is its general usage in Scripture, as in Prov. 5 [3, 9]: "Honor the Lord with your substance." And Luke 8, 43: "She paid out all her substance to physicians." And I John 3, 17: "If any one has the substance of this world and sees his brother in need [how does God's love abide in him]." ...Chrysostom, however, interprets "substance" in a different way from St. Jerome, taking it to mean "essence" or "underlying reality." ...Although the later interpretation of "substance" [as essence] does not seem appropriate for understanding the definition of faith below in chapter 11, because there, "substance of things hoped for," suggests only the former interpretation of "substance" as the possession of goods, nevertheless it does fit here. Therefore, let us bring both interpretations together, because through faith Christ is called our "substance," that is, our riches, and at the same time and through the same faith we become his "substance," that is, a new creature.[47]

Faith as "substance" means that through faith man possesses Christ and likewise Christ possesses the believer. In stark contrast then to medieval exegetes who define faith as the beginning of a process of adding love and hope to faith, faith as "possession" means for Luther

---

[44] Tarantasia, p. 184.

[45] Lyra, p. 139v; Dionysius the Carthusian, p. 484.

[46] Faber Stapulensis, p. 234v.

[47] WA 57. III. 152. 1-153. 10.

that salvation is complete and full to one who has faith. Faith is the
first, last, and only step towards salvation. What for medieval theology
was future and belonged only to the realm of hope and love, Luther
regards a reality in the present. Faith is not of one's own doing or of
one's own nature, yet it is really one's own "possession."[48]

By defining faith as *possessio* Luther is in disagreement with medieval
exegetes who define faith as *fides formata*. Bizer, however, claims that
Luther in his exegesis of 5, 1 is still thinking of faith in terms of *fides
formata* and justification as the impartation of righteousness, because
faith means the purity of the heart—"faith (*effektiv*) makes the heart
clean."[49] But Luther cannot be thinking of faith as *fides formata* in
5, 1 and later,[50] when, in his interpretation of 3, 14 as we have seen
in the light of medieval exegesis, Luther rejects the medieval understanding of "substance" (faith) as the "foundation" of doing works
of love.

Bizer and Gyllenkrok both regard any language on Luther's part
which suggests the impartation of righteousness to the believer as a
pre-Reformation stage of Luther's development—Luther's *Turmerlebnis* occurs when Luther discovers that the Word does not give
righteousness but promises salvation.[51] Gyllenkrok holds that Luther
has arrived at his Reformation understanding of "promise" by the
time of his *Lectures on Hebrews*.[52] But in his exegesis of 3, 12 Luther
clearly says that man is given righteousness and becomes pure and
good:

> Faith in the Word purifies, because, just as the Word of God is completely pure
> and good, so he who adheres to it becomes like the Word, pure and good. In
> general, whatever the Word possesses and is able to give, it shares with him who
> adheres to it and believes it.[53]

Bizer holds that Luther is scholastic in his exegesis of 7, 1 because
he speaks of imparted righteousness. Reinhard Schwarz argues that

---

[48] Luther's understanding of faith as *possessio* in his *Lectures on Hebrews* supports
Oberman's argument based on the *Disputatio de Iustificatione* (1536), that *possessio*
stands in contrast to *proprietas*. (Heiko A. Oberman, " 'Iustitia Christi' and 'Iustitia
Dei.' Luther and the Scholastic Doctrines of Justification," *Harvard Theological Review*
59 [1966], pp. 21-22).

[49] Bizer, *Fides ex auditu*, pp. 81, 91.

[50] *Ibid.*, p. 93.

[51] *Ibid.*, p. 172; Gyllenkrok, *Rechtfertigung und Heiligung*, p. 75.

[52] Gyllenkrok, pp. 72, 75.

[53] *WA* 57. III. 147. 20-148. 2.

Luther in his exegesis of 3, 12-13 is anti-scholastic because for Luther faith which makes man "pure and good" is not a *virtus* or a quality, the first of the three spiritual virtues, but is conformity with the *verbum Dei*, the Son of God.[54]

Without raising or solving the *Turmerlebnis* problem it can be said that Luther in the context of 3, 12, 14 and later understands faith as the possession of salvation. This means that man is given righteousness not as a habit but as constitutive of his relation to God which is that he "becomes like the Word, pure and good."

11,1. "Now faith is the substance of things hoped for, the evidence of things not seen."

Luther explicitly discusses two interpretations of 11, 1 given in the Middle Ages and then offers a third alternative. At stake is the definition of faith and the interpretation of faith as "substance" (*substantia*) and "evidence" (*argumentum*).

Luther singles out Chrysostom's interpretation as one alternative. Luther correctly reports that "substance" for Chrysostom means "essence" (*essentia*) or "underlying reality" (*subsistentia*). Faith for Chrysostom makes "the things hoped for" real to the believer and gives them their substance and reality. Chrysostom says:

> If the "things hoped for" are thought to be without substance, faith gives them their substance. However, it would be better to say that faith does not give substance to these things, but is in fact their very essence. For example, the resurrection has not yet occurred nor is there yet any substance to it, but hope makes it exist in our soul. This is what "substance" means.[55]

In his discussion of faith as "the conviction of things not seen" Chrysostom says that faith is the *visio* of things not apparent and that this *visio* leads the believer to the same assurance (*satisfactio*) as "things seen" convey, in fact, more so. The "just live by faith," seeing the things of God not visibly seen by the eye. Luther cites Chrysostom:

> And again Chrysostom: "What a wonderful word is used when he says: 'Conviction of things not seen.' For there is only conviction with regard to visible things. Therefore faith is the vision of things not seen."[56]

[54] *Fides, Spes und Caritas beim jungen Luther unter besonderer Berücksichtigung der mittelalterlichen Tradition* (Berlin, 1962), pp. 302-306.

[55] Chrysostom, p. 369.

[56] *WA* 57. III. 228. 8-10.

Chrysostom's general interpretation of faith regarding c. 11 is that reason can never discover the *maximae res* that are attained through faith.[57] Human reasoning is weak. The acts of faith by the great patriarchs of the Old Testament were above, beyond and contrary to the power of reason.[58] Reason would never suggest what faith did. In short, "by faith" in c. 11 means for Chrysostom, not by reason, because "things seen" are subject to sense experience and thus to reason, whereas faith is the *visio* of "things not seen."

The other interpretation of 11, 1 discussed by Luther is that given by "some" who interpret "substance" as "cause" or "foundation":

> Some interpret "substance" to mean "cause" or "foundation."... "Evidence," for these same interpreters, is understood to mean "proof," "conviction" and everything which is considered to be "evidence" in dialectics, so that there is some certainty that "things not seen" do exist, namely, "things" the patriarchs and other saints believed.[59]

These "some" include the *Glossa interlinearis* and *Glossa ordinaria*, Aquinas, Tarantasia, Lyra, Burgos and Faber Stapulensis.

Faith as "substance" is interpreted by the *Glossa* to be the "foundation" and "cause" of "all good." It is the *sine qua non* of a "good edifice." Faith as "evidence" is interpreted as the "certitude" and "proof" of the hope of resurrection. The "proof" is that the Old Testament patriarchs, the Apostles and other saints had such a faith.[60]

The remainder of c. 11 is interpreted by the *Glossa ordinaria* as a praise of the exemplary faith and life of the Old Testament patriarchs. The nature of their faith is assumed, and attention rather focuses on what they did.

In the context of 3, 14 and 6, 1, Aquinas defines faith as "substance" to be the "foundation" of virtue and works of love. Aquinas' exegesis of 11, 1 is a discussion of his definition of a virtue or a habit, its "act" and "object." The virtue of faith is "an act of the intellect" (*assensus*) moved "by the command of the will." The "object" of faith is the "end" of the intellect and the will, namely, "truth" and "the good." In short, Aquinas says, "faith is a habit of the mind by which eternal life is begun in us, making the intellect assent to things not seen."[61]

---

[57] Chrysostom, p. 372.

[58] *Ibid.*, p. 389.

[59] *WA* 57. III. 226. 10-227. 1.

[60] *Glossa interlinearis*, f. 154r-154v.

[61] Aquinas, pp. 457-59.

Tarantasia and Burgos say that faith as "substance" is the "cause" of hope. Faith as "evidence" is the "proof" or "demonstration" of "things not seen."[62] The "evidence" or "argument," says Tarantasia, is that "the fathers believed, therefore we conclude that it is so."

Lyra, like Aquinas, defines faith as an intellectual act (*assensus*) derived "from the command of the will" and directed towards "truth" and "the good" as its object. Also like Aquinas, faith for Lyra is the first of the virtues—*prima virtus infusa*—and the "beginning"of works performed in love for the purpose of attaining final beatitude. Faith is the "habit of the mind by which eternal life is begun in us, making the intellect assent to things not seen."[63]

At the end of his discussion of chapter 5, Lyra distinguishes between two levels of faith. He holds that certain "mysteries of the faith" are believed by all "explicitly through simple assent," such as the incarnation, passion and resurrection of Christ and similar doctrines which are generally preached in the Church. For the "simple" to be "in fulness of faith" it is necessary that they believe what the Church believes.[64] The other level of faith applies to the "superiores." The "subtle aspects of the faith"—the "rationale" of Christian doctrine and the implications of the "mysteries of the faith"—are held by "only those who are *superiores* in the Church and such things are not discussed with the simple."[65]

Faber Stapulensis, like the *Glossa ordinaria*, Aquinas and Lyra, holds that faith as "substance" is the "foundation" of the virtues. Faith is the "sustenance, support, and foundation of hope." It is the "foundation of life, the support of hope and the anchor of love."[66]

Luther opposes these medieval exegetes who define "substance" as "foundation" and "evidence" as "proof." Luther says, regarding "some" who define "substance" as "foundation":

> It is certainly true that faith is "the foundation of the Apostles and prophets" upon which, according to the apostle in Eph. 2, 20, we are "built." And I Cor. 3, 11: "The foundation which is laid." Just as Christ himself says in Matt. 16, 18: "Upon this rock I will build my Church," that is, upon the stability of faith. But whether "substance" is to be taken in this way or not, we will leave to others.[67]

---

[62] Tarantasia, p. 248; Burgos, f. 158r.

[63] Lyra, f. 154v.

[64] *Ibid.*, f. 153r.

[65] *Ibid.*, f. 142v-143r.

[66] Faber Stapulensis, f. 253r-253v.

[67] *WA* 57. III. 226. 11-17.

Luther's understanding of faith as "possessio" prohibits his understanding faith as the "foundation" of a virtuous life.

Luther's opposition to the definition of "evidence" as "proof" is not
as charitable:

> This position does not please me, because it would follow that Adam and Abel
> did not have faith, because they could not draw certainty from the fact that
> others had believed before them, since they were the first in faith. This position
> also seems to contradict itself. For according to this interpretation faith would
> be nothing other than belief based on the persuasion and proof of another's belief.[68]

Luther's own position is that "substance" throughout Scripture
means "possession":

> Thirdly, let us follow the most common use of "substance." In Scripture, it almost
> always means possession and supply, as in Heb. 10, 34: "You knew that you
> yourself had a better and an abiding substance." And Luke 8:43: "She had paid
> out all her substance to physicians." And I John 3:17: "If any one has the substance
> of this world."[69]

In his discussion of Heb. 11, 1 in his *Dictata* Luther also defines faith
as "substance" to be *possessio* of future things hoped for.[70]

The striking aspects about Luther's understanding of faith as
possessio are, first of all, its different emphasis from the *"visio* theology" of Chrysostom and the *"intellectus* theology" of Aquinas and
Lyra, and, secondly, its opposition to the understanding of faith as
the "foundation" of the virtues.

Faith as *possessio* means for Luther that when one "hears" the
Word or "adheres" to it, justification is complete and full. Faith as
"substance" is the possession of the Word:

> Therefore, since faith is nothing other than adherence to the Word of God, as
> in Rom. 1, it follows that faith is at the same time the possession of the Word
> of God—of eternal goods—and the removal of all present goods, at least as far
> as one's devotion and adherence to them goes.[71]

For Luther, one possesses the Word by "hearing" it. For Chrysostom,
on the other hand, faith is "seeing" "things not seen." And for Aquinas
and Lyra, faith is an "act of the intellect."

In his theology of testament in the *Dictata*, Luther refers often to

---

[68] *WA* 57. III. 227. 1-5.
[69] *WA* 57. III. 228. 11-15.
[70] *WA* 3. 419. 25-420. 13; cf. *WA* 4. 271. 29-31.
[71] *WA* 57. III. 228. 17-20.

Heb. 11, 1 in order to specify the way the Word of the Lord, as law, as gospel, is received. Luther defines "my testament"(Ps. 49, 16) as "the Word of God which testifies to us about future and invisible realities." [72] In this life, at any point in time, we believe not in *rem ipsam* but in *argumentum non apparentium*. The Word is "a testimony to the eternal realities themselves." [73] The testament is a *pactum fidei* (Ps. 73, 20).[74]

D. Personal Certitude of Salvation

5,1. "For every high priest chosen from among men is appointed to act for men in relation to God, to offer gifts and sacrifices for sins."

Luther begins his exegesis of 5, 1 by saying that the emphasis of the verse is on the phrase, "for men."[75] The importance of the phrase for Luther distinguishes between a general or objective knowledge of Christ's work "for men" and a particular or subjective certainty that Christ's work "for men" means salvation for "me," a striking distinction in the light of medieval exegesis.

Alcuin says that the office of a priest involves standing between God and man and interceding for "his beloved people." This is what Christ did by offering himself "for our sins," living "for us" and always interceding "for men."[76]

The *Glossa interlinearis*, Aquinas and Tarantasia direct little attention to the phrase. The *Glossa interlinearis* says that a priest works " 'for men,' so that they might obtain mercy from God through him."[77] Aquinas says that a priest is not appointed for his own glory or wealth but "for the utility of men."[78] Tarantasia says that a priest is concerned not "for oxen," but "for men," for their salvation and not their temporal welfare.[79]

Faber Stapulensis goes on at great length comparing Christ and

---

[72] *WA* 3. 279. 8-9.
[73] *WA* 3. 279. 30-33.
[74] *WA* 3. 491. 10-11: " 'Respice' miserendo 'in testamentum tuum' pactum scil. fidei et evangelii, quia eternum est, ut rursum refloreat et prevaleat."
[75] *WA* 57. III. 165. 15.
[76] Alcuin, p. 1052.
[77] *Glossa interlinearis*, f. 141v-142r.
[78] Aquinas (5, 1), pp. 389-90.
[79] Tarantasia (5, 1), p. 193.

the priests of the Old Testament. The Old Testament priests offered sacrifices both for themselves and for others, whereas Christ who was without sin offered himself only "for others." Christ's one sacrifice "for the sins of all" was "potentior" and, in fact, the only true one because it was "a sacrifice for the whole world."[80]

Luther says that anyone, even the demons and the godless, knows that Christ was a high priest "for men," however this knowledge must not be confused with faith. For faith is believing with certainty that one personally is among those for whom Christ is high priest. Whereas medieval exegetes, particularly Alcuin and Faber Stapulensis, emphasize that Christ is truly a high priest "for men," Luther argues that faith is the personal certainty of salvation "for me." Faith for Luther is the confident trust that one's own sins are forgiven and that one will assuredly be given eternal life:

> We should note that it is not sufficient for a Christian to believe that Christ was appointed for men unless he believes that he himself is one of them. For also the demons and godless know that Christ is high priest for men, but they do not believe that they are among such men. Thus the sum and substance of St. Bernard's sermon on the Annunciation (the theme of which is, "That glory may dwell in our land"): it is necessary that you believe that God is able to forgive your sins, confer grace upon you and give glory to you. However, this is not sufficient unless you believe with the most certain faith that it is your sins that are forgiven, that grace is conferred upon you and that glory will be given to you.[81]

9,24. "For Christ has entered, not into a sanctuary made with hands, a copy of the true one, but into heaven itself, to appear in the presence of God on our behalf."

Luther begins his exegesis of 9, 24 by discussing the significance of the phrase, "on our behalf," for the personal certitude of salvation. He differentiates between two ways of knowing God—"speculatively" or objectively, and "practically" or subjectively. Though the latter is the only adequate way for Luther, the former way is strikingly similar to the theology represented in medieval exegesis of 9, 24.

Chrysostom, the *Glossa ordinaria*, Aquinas and Tarantasia devote their exegesis of 9, 24 to a comparison between the two Testaments, especially a comparison between the two sacrifices. A predominant characteristic of Christ's sacrifice for these medieval exegetes as well as for Lyra is that it was "on our behalf." Chrysostom asks, "What

---

[80] Faber Stapulensis (C. 5), f. 237r.

[81] *WA* 57. III. 169. 10-18.

is 'on our behalf?' He went up, he means, with a sacrifice which had power to appease the Father."[82] The *Glossa ordinaria* says that through Christ's sacrifice, which was "better" than those of the Old Testament, he entered into heaven for us in order to intercede for us.[83] Aquinas interprets the phrase "on our behalf" to refer to Christ's ascension "in order to prepare the way for us.... For the body ought to follow its head."[84] Tarantasia says that Christ intercedes for us "and thus cleanses the Church from ignorance, poverty, and malice."[85] Lyra says that Christ represents the humanity which he assumed for us.[86]

For all these exegetes Christ's "appearing in the presence of God on our behalf" refers to Christ's self offer and intercession for the salvation of all mankind. This kind of thinking for Luther is "speculative" knowledge available to all. It is knowledge about the historical facts of salvation but it is not true faith. For Luther it is one thing to know about Christ's work "on our behalf" and another to believe with certainty that "I" personally am one of those for whom Christ is priest and intercedes:

> It has been said that some know Christ speculatively, some practically. The former believe that Christ appeared in the presence of God for some, whereas the latter believe that Christ appeared in the presence of God for us. Therefore, it is necessary that a Christian be certain, in fact absolutely certain, that Christ appeared for him, and is his high priest before God. As one believes so it happens to him.[87]

E. Conclusion

Faith for Luther is the possession "of eternal goods," given by the "eternum testamentum."[88] As seen above, one who hears the Word becomes like the Word, good, pure, and just. However, for medieval exegetes, faith, an infused habit, is only the first of the virtues, a necessary foundation but only a foundation which demands the completion of a good building, the development of one's life.

---

[82] Chrysostom, p. 346-47.
[83] *Glossa ordinaria*, f. 151r-151v.
[84] Aquinas (9, 24), pp. 438-39.
[85] Tarantasia, p. 233.
[86] Lyra, f. 151v.
[87] *WA* 57. III. 215. 16-20.
[88] *WA* 4. 193. 20-21.

Faith as possession for Luther is more than the imputation of righteousness, for one is made good, pure and just. But faith is not an infused habit. Faith is "hearing" the Word, being "clean" and just, having salvation in the present, and the certitude of salvation.

CHAPTER FOUR

CHRISTOLOGY

In his Introduction and elsewhere, Luther states that Paul, in Hebrews, has something important to say about Christ and the Old Testament. In his Christological concern, what comes to the fore in the light of medieval exegesis is the strong soteriological emphasis Luther gives to the variety of Christological texts in Hebrews. By way of the lowly humanity of Christ (1, 2 and 2, 7) there is purgation without penance (1, 3) of a people who are led by no other staff (1, 8 and 1, 9). By way of faith conformity is constituted (2, 10). Christ, a priest without comparison (5, 1 and 5, 6), offers his testament for the forgiveness of sins (9, 17). Christ leveled the rough road and holds out his hand in order to elicit our confidence. As sacrament and example he made it possible for us to die confidently (10, 19).

A. By Way of Lowly Humanity

1,2. "But in these last days he has spoken to us by his Son, whom he appointed the heir of all things, through whom he made the worlds also."

When one reads medieval exegetes, two aspects of Luther's exegesis of 1, 2 stand out.

One is the fact that Luther deals with a distinction between the humanity and the divinity of Christ which was made in various ways in the Middle Ages:

> He describes the same Christ as the Son of man and the Son of God. The phrase "he was appointed the heir of all things," relates particularly to his humanity, whereas the phrase "the worlds were made through him," relates to his divinity.[1]

Tarantasia and Lyra make the same distinction between the humanity and the divinity of Christ—the phrase, "he was appointed the heir of all things" refers to the humanity, and the phrase, "the worlds were made through him" refers to the divinity.[2] The *Glossa inter-*

---

[1] *WA* 57. III. 98. 12-15.

[2] Tarantasia, p. 164; Lyra, f. 133v.

linearis, however, offers a different interpretation. Both phrases refer to the humanity of Christ, whereas v. 3 ("He is the brightness of his glory and the figure of his substance") applies to the divinity of Christ.[3] Pseudo-Hugh of St. Victor and Aquinas understand the verse in still another way. The phrase, "heir of all things" applies to both the humanity and divinity of Christ.[4]

Although Luther makes the same distinction between the humanity and the divinity of Christ as Tarantasia and Lyra do, the soteriological implication which Luther draws from his distinction is one not made by his exegetical predecessors but one which is striking because of Chrysostom's discussion of 1, 2-4. This distinction is the second aspect of Luther's exegesis of 1, 2 which stands out in the light of medieval exegesis.

Luther says that the importance of the fact that the humanity of Christ is mentioned before his divinity is that the only way to God is through the humanity of Christ:

> We should note here that he mentions the humanity of Christ before his divinity, and thus he affirms the rule for knowing God by way of faith. For the humanity is that holy ladder by which we ascend to the knowledge of God (Gen. 28). Thus also, John 6 [14, 6]: "No one comes to the Father, but by me." Or: "I am the door" (John 10, 7). He who wishes to ascend vigorously to the love and knowledge of God must abandon the human and metaphysical rules concerning knowledge of divinity and apply himself first to the humanity of Christ. For it is the most scandalous temerity that whereas God has humiliated himself in order to become understood, man would look for another road, relying on insights of his own.[5]

In contrast to Luther's reference to the humanity of Christ as "that holy ladder by which we ascend to the knowledge of God," Chrysostom interprets 1, 2-4 as a series of steps (*gradus*) or levels of discourse which describe the person of Christ. These "degrees of ascent" range from the "humble" matters discussed in v. 2 up to the "unapproachable light" of Christ's brightness (v. 3) and down again "to what is lowly" (v. 4).[6]

Chrysostom like other medieval exegetes concentrates on the lowly and exalted aspects of the person of Christ, whereas Luther emphasizes the significance of the person of Christ for the work of salvation.

---

[3] *Glossa interlinearis,* f. 133v-134r.

[4] Ps.-Hugh of St. Victor, p. 610; Aquinas, p. 340.

[5] *WA* 57. III. 99. 1-10.

[6] Chrysostom, pp. 238-39.

Knowledge of Christ's nature is inadequate. One must experience or "apply (*exerceat*) himself to the humanity of Christ" in faith.

2,7. "Thou didst make him a little lower than the angels, thou hast crowned him with glory and honor."

Luther specifically discusses how his interpretation of Christ's humiliation in 2, 7 differs from other interpretations. He describes four positions taken by his predecessors and his opposition to each. An independent study of these exegetes reveals that Luther is actually in agreement with Chrysostom whom he explicitly opposes and with Aquinas whom he implicitly attacks.

The first position, extensively and strongly opposed by Luther, is that taken by "a great many doctors, especially Jerome, and at times also Augustine, Ambrose and Chrysostom.[7] Their interpretation, according to Luther, is that the person who was made "a little lower than the angels" is man. Thus for these doctors, says Luther, "this verse refers to the dignity of human nature, because it is nearest to the angels." The difficulty with this position for Luther is that 2, 7 can only be interpreted to refer to Christ. Otherwise the context is distorted.[8] Luther's criticism is in accord with medieval exegetes who, from Chrysostom to Erasmus, interpret 2, 7 as referring to the incarnate Christ.

The second position, briefly dismissed by Luther as "not precise enough,"[9] is the interpretation of 2, 7 given throughout the medieval exegetical tradition. Luther's objection to this position has to do with its interpretation of the phrase "a little lower." Medieval exegetes offer various explanations of this phrase. It was interpreted by Chrysostom to refer to the three days Christ spent in Hades,[10] by Alcuin to refer to Christ's "mortal body,"[11] by the *Glossa interlinearis* to refer to Christ's "passible nature,"[12] by Pseudo-Hugh of St. Victor to refer to the "weakness" of Christ's flesh,[13] by Aquinas to refer, first of all, not to Christ's soul but to his body which is capable of suffering and, secondly, to the short duration of his suffering and

---

[7] *WA* 57. III. 116. 8-10.

[8] *WA* 57. III. 116. 8-117. 6.

[9] *WA* 57. III. 117. 6-10.

[10] Chrysostom, pp. 263-64.

[11] Alcuin, p. 1040.

[12] *Glossa interlinearis*, f. 137r.

[13] Ps.-Hugh of St. Victor, pp. 614-15.

death,[14] and by Tarantasia and Lyra to refer to Christ's "passible nature."[15]

Luther refers to this medieval interpretation of 2, 7 simply as the position of "others" who "understand this verse to refer to Christ as being lower than the angels, not according to his soul but according to his body which is capable of suffering." The position which Luther describes is specifically that of Aquinas, though similar to the other medieval exegetes. Luther's information undoubtedly comes from Erasmus, who discusses Aquinas' interpretation at length, since there is no evidence that Luther worked directly with Aquinas' commentary on Hebrews.[16]

Not only is Luther's description of the position of "others" similar to Erasmus' discussion of Aquinas, but Luther's refutation of this position is also similar to Erasmus' argument against Aquinas' position. Erasmus' and Luther's objection to this position is that Christ was made not only partially "a little lower than the angels," but completely and totally lower than even "the most abject of men" (Is. 53, 3). They both cite Ps. 21, 7 as referring to Christ: "I am a worm, and not a man."

The third position described by Luther is that of Faber Stapulensis. Faber Stapulensis argues that Paul wrote to the Hebrews in their language and that Paul, who is quoting from Ps. 8, 5 in Heb. 2, 7, undoubtedly would have followed the Hebrew reading of Ps. 8, 5, which is that "Christ was made a little lower than God (*Elohim*)." The Greek translator of Paul's epistle took his reading of Ps. 8, 5 from the LXX, which reads: "Christ was made a little lower than the angels (*Malachim*)." Paul was mis-translated at this point for the original Hebrew simply refers to Christ's exinanition.[17]

For his objections to Faber Stapulensis' interpretation, Luther again draws upon Erasmus. Luther first cites, for the second time, Erasmus' objection to Aquinas' interpretation—Christ was made not only "a little lower than God" but also "lower than the most abject of men." Luther then cites Erasmus' argument about the meaning of *Elohim* saying, "that 'Elohim' in Hebrew means not only God

---

[14] Aquinas, pp. 361-62.
[15] Tarantasia, p. 173; Lyra, f. 137r.
[16] Erasmus, pp. 585-86.
[17] Faber Stapulensis, f. 233v.

but also angels, and in fact high court officials and anyone holding a position of power."[18]

Finally, Luther states his own interpretation over against the position of Erasmus. Erasmus' argument is "that the phrase, 'a little lower,' does not refer to the measure of diminished dignity, but to the brief time during which Christ lived on this earth." Such an interpretation, claims Erasmus, is similar to Chrysostom (who speaks of the three days in Hades) and Aquinas (who speaks of the short duration of Christ's suffering and death).

Luther's objection to Erasmus' interpretation is that Erasmus has misunderstood the verb "to make lower." Erasmus understands the verb to refer to the duration of Christ's life. For Luther it refers to God's abandonment of Christ during the three days of his death:

> Thus the meaning is this: thou didst allow him to be forsaken and deserted by God or the angels, not for a long time but for a very little while, indeed less than a little while, that is, for the briefest time possible, namely, for three days, because thou didst hand him over into the hand of sinners.[19]

In his *Dictata* Luther does not speak in terms of the three days but in terms of Christ's total exinanition according to both natures, a position which was later to be espoused by Erasmus and rejected by Luther.[20]

As the argument turns out, Chrysostom and Aquinas are misplaced persons in both Erasmus' and Luther's arguments. Luther categorizes Chrysostom under the first group who identify the person made "a little lower" as man. Erasmus claims Chrysostom for his position. Actually, Chrysostom and Luther agree that 2, 7 refers to the short duration of Christ's descent into Hell.

The second position which Luther attacks is one half of Aquinas' interpretation—that Christ was made lower than the angels according to his passible body, not according to his soul. Both Erasmus and Luther oppose this interpretation because it undermines the complete character of Christ's exinanition. They both quote Ps. 21, 7 in support of their argument: "I am a worm and not a man." However, Aquinas also cites this verse as well as Is. 54, 7 in the second half of his explanation in order to show the total proportions of Christ's humiliation

---

[18] *WA* 57. III. 117. 10-118. 8.

[19] *WA* 57. III. 118. 8-119. 9.

[20] *WA* 55. I. 62. 2-9, 20-24.

during his passion and death. Luther also argues that Heb. 2, 7 "has the same meaning as Is. 54, 7-8":

> We conclude, therefore, that our text, "Thou didst make him for a short time lower than the angels, [thou hast crowned him] with glory and honor," has the same meaning as Is. 54, 7-8: "For a brief moment I forsook you, but with great compassion I will gather you. And in a moment of indignation I hid my face a little while from you, but with everlasting love I will have compassion on you."[21]

Erasmus, then, who inappropriately claims Chrysostom and Aquinas for his side, is opposed by Luther, who actually is in agreement with Chrysostom and Aquinas though Luther explicitly opposes Chrysostom and implicitly takes exception to the first half of Aquinas' position.

Luther is concerned to emphasize that God totally humiliated himself in the death of Christ. Knowledge of the person of Christ is useless for salvation. Christ is a "worm" so that God could be understood.

B. Purgation Without Penance

1,3.   "He is the brightness of his glory and the figure of his substance, upholding all things by the word of his power. When he made purgation of sins he sat down at the right hand of the Majesty on high."

There are many similarities between Luther's exegesis of 1, 3a ("He is the brightness of his glory and the figure of his substance") and his medieval predecessors. In his analysis of this sentence Luther displays a philological interest which is more akin to Valla, Faber Stapulensis, and Erasmus than to the traditional interest in the Son's relation to the Father.[22]

Luther concentrates on the meaning and translation of the words "brightness," "glory," "figure," and "substance." He draws heavily on his predecessors. Luther's entire Gloss is taken from various medieval exegetes, namely, the *Glossa interlinearis*, Chrysostom, the *Glossa ordinaria* and Burgos.[23] In his Scholium Luther's explanation of the meaning of "brightness" as "brilliance" comes from Erasmus.[24] His

---

[21] *WA* 57. III. 119. 9-16.

[22] *WA* 57. III. 99. 12-101-2; Valla, p. 885; Faber Stapulensis, f. 231r-231v; Erasmus, pp. 584-55.

[23] Chrysostom, pp. 244-46; *Glossa ordinaria*, f. 134r; Burgos, f. 136r.

[24] *WA* 57. III. 99. 15.

description of "brightness" as "the image of his glory" is similar
to Lyra's definition of "the figure of his substance."[25] Luther defines
the meaning of the phrase, "the figure of his substance" on the basis
of the Greek text. His translation of the Greek is similar to Faber
Stapulensis' and Erasmus'.

What is striking about Luther's exegesis of 1, 3 is his lack of
interest in the Trinitarian issues raised by medieval exegetes:

> It is not necessary to argue, as some do, that "the brightness of his glory" refers
> to a personal distinction and "the figure of his substance" to a substantial unity.
> In each case both are expressed.[26]

Chrysostom devotes an entire Homily to the Trinitarian implications
of 1, 3. He is concerned to show that this verse excludes the errors of
Sabellianism and Arianism. The Son and the Father are *duae subsistentiae*. The *Glossa ordinaria*, Pseudo-Hugh of St. Victor, Aquinas,
Lyra, and Burgos continue along the same lines as Chrysostom,
emphasizing at length that the Son is co-eternal and consubstantial
with the Father.[27]

Luther's exegesis of 1, 3c ("When he made purgation of sins he
sat down at the right hand of the Majesty on high") is far from
traditional. Aquinas and Lyra interpret 1, 3c with the same Trinitarian interests as 1, 3a. For Aquinas and Lyra, 1, 3c shows that
Christ is equal in power with the Father. Chrysostom says briefly that
1, 3c shows Christ's care and concern for man.[28] Faber Stapulensis
recounts the story of the healing of the paralytic as an example that
Christ did accomplish the forgiveness of sins.[29]

Luther displays a strong and specific soteriological interest: "In
this one phrase ['when he made purgation of sins'] [Paul] reduces
all the righteousness and penitence of man to utter futility."[30] This
means that human efforts to achieve forgiveness are inadequate because
repentance and forgiveness are totally the works of Christ:

> We should, therefore, despair of our penance, of our purgation of sins, because
> before we come to penance, our sins are already forgiven, in fact his very purgation
> first effects penance in us, just as his righteousness effects our righteousness.[31]

---

25 Lyra, f. 134r.
26 *WA* 57. III. 100. 2-5.
27 Ps.-Hugh of St. Victor, p. 610; Aquinas, p. 343.
28 Chrysostom, p. 247.
29 Faber Stapulensis, f. 231r.
30 *WA* 57. III. 101. 16-17.
31 *WA* 57. III. 101. 19-22.

Luther's strong soteriological interest differentiates him from Chrysostom, Aquinas, and Lyra. Luther's specific soteriological point that
Christ accomplishes salvation in man apart from man's penance
differentiates Luther from Faber Stapulensis and his more historical
interest.

C. A ROYAL PEOPLE BY NO OTHER STAFF

1,8. "But of the Son he says, 'Thy throne, O God, is for ever and
ever, a staff of justice is the staff of thy kingdom.' "

Luther's exegesis of 1, 8 (Ps. 44, 7) is different from the medieval
exegetical tradition, though this is not apparent from what he says.
The difference lies in the contrasting interpretations of the words
"throne" and "staff," which in turn are related to contrasting interpretations of the word "justice" in v. 9.

Medieval exegetes, beginning with Alcuin, interpret "throne" as
the seat or locus of judgment. Chrysostom interprets 1, 8-9 as a
refutation of the Trinitarian errors of the Jews, Paul of Samosata,
the Arians, Marcellus, Sabellius and Marcion. In opposition against
such errors Chrysostom argues that the Son and the Father are "two
persons distinguished in reference to their subsistence."[32] Faber Stapulensis interprets the verse along the same lines, arguing against
the Jews that Christ is true man and true God.[33] Faber Stapulensis
and Chrysostom are interested in the fact that the verse says that
Christ is "God" and that his throne "is for ever and ever." Other
medieval exegetes concentrate on the meaning of the word "throne."
Alcuin, the *Glossa interlinearis*, Aquinas, Tarantasia and Dionysius
the Carthusian argue that the word "throne" refers to the seat of
judgment occupied by Christ.[34] For God has given all judgment to
his Son. Christ is the judge of the living and the dead. Christ as judge
rules and directs his kingdom with his "staff."

Christ's "staff" is interpreted by Alcuin, the *Glossa interlinearis*,
Tarantasia and Dionysius the Carthusian to mean discipline.[35] Christ

---

[32] Chrysostom, pp. 252-53.

[33] Faber Stapulensis, f. 231v.

[34] Alcuin, p. 1036; *Glossa interlinearis*, f. 135r; Aquinas, pp. 348-49; Tarantasia,
p. 167; Dionysius the Carthusian, p. 475.

[35] Alcuin, p. 1036; *Glossa interlinearis*, f. 135r; Tarantasia, p. 167; Dionysius the
Carthusian, p. 475.

rules his kingdom with just, fair, and inflexible discipline. Christ's "staff" is a *directa regula*, an inflexible standard whereby the evil are persecuted and the just exalted.

Luther interprets 1, 8 quite differently. Luther understands "throne" to mean the Church, a royal people, both in his *Dictata* and in his *Lectures on Hebrews*.[36] Luther stresses the differences between the appearance of this people and their reality. Though they are a priestly, royal and holy people in reality, in appearance they seem quite the contrary:

> For if considered according to its appearance, nothing is less related to a throne, especially to the throne of God, than the people of Christ, since they do not appear to be a kingdom but to be in exile, not to be living but constantly dying, not to be in glory but in disgrace, not to live in wealth but in extreme poverty. Thus everyone who wants to become a member of this kingdom is compelled to experience these things for himself.[37]

The existence of this people—in exile, disgrace, and poverty— seems to contradict their reality. Elsewhere in his lectures Luther describes the Church as *intermixta*:

> The Church is made up of various believers from all over the world and is intermixed with many helpless, imperfect and sinful people, as Christ says in John 12, 8: "The poor you will always have with you, but you will not always have me."[38]

The royal people of Christ, though in exile and intermixed with sinners, are ruled and protected by the "staff" of God. Luther interprets the word "staff" to mean the gospel of the Word of God, both in his *Dictata*[39] and in his *Lectures on Hebrews*. In these lectures he says that the people are directed (*dirigo*) by the Word and thus live under the gospel and not under discipline:

> It seems certain, therefore, that this "staff," as others interpret it, is inflexible power, but actually it is nothing other than the gospel itself or the Word of God. For Christ rules the Church by no other power than the Word.[40]

In the light of medieval exegesis Luther's attack on other staffs, other doctrines and good behavior begins to make sense. Luther is implicitly opposing those medieval exegetes who interpreted "staff"

---

[36] *WA* 3. 251. 5-8; cf. *WA* 57. III. 107. 11, 17.

[37] *WA* 57. III. 107. 15-108. 1.

[38] *WA* 57. III. 224. 18-21.

[39] *WA* 3. 251. 5-8.

[40] *WA* 57. III. 108. 15-109. 1.

as discipline which is concerned with making men good. Luther is suspicious of good behavior and virtue because man basically loves himself. The gospel for Luther attacks and destroys the old man:

> And thus the gospel retains nothing of the old man but destroys everything and makes everything new, so that inward love of himself becomes hatred of himself through faith in Christ.[41]

The Church is ruled only by the gospel, for any other staff is "crooked and unjust."[42] Man is made new only through the gospel:

> No other doctrine, either civil or ecclesiastical or philosophical, is in any way able to direct man and make him upright, even if it leads him in such a manner that it establishes good behavior.[43]

Both in his *Dictata* and in his *Lectures on Hebrews*, Luther emphasizes that the "staff" radically makes men "straight" (*dirigo*). This *directio* means that "the carnal and old man 'is broken into pieces like a potter's vessel' (Ps. 2, 9),"[44] or, as the *Dictata* has it: the gospel "disciplines the undisciplined," "humiliates the proud," "bends down the high-and-mighty," "shatters the presumptuous" and so forth.[45] The *directio* of the "staff" also "makes everything new through faith in Christ," or in the words of the *Dictata*: the gospel "soothes the harsh (that is, tempers the wrathful), lengthens the short (that is, makes the fearful mighty in spirit)."[46] In another discussion of *virga* in his *Dictata*, Luther says:

> Corollary: it follows that this power is not carnal and against men according to the flesh, but it is spiritual and that which fights against sins and evils and the workers of evils—namely, men and devils. And this is the very grace of God, which is conferred on us in the words of the Gospel.... The staff is the same as the sword, the grace is the same as the power, for the grace of God overcomes all sins, sinners, and demons, either converting them or rendering them harmless.[47]

Elsewhere in his *Lectures on Hebrews* Luther emphasizes that the people of Christ who live under the gospel alone are protected from harm by the Word alone:

> Is. 27, 2-4: "In that day: a pleasant vineyard, sing of it! I, the Lord, am its keeper;

---

41 *WA* 57. III. 109. 17-19.
42 *WA* 57. III. 109. 8.
43 *WA* 57. III. 109. 9-12.
44 *WA* 57. III. 108. 9-11.
45 *WA* 55. II. 37. 19ff.
46 *WA* 55. II. 39. 2-4.
47 *WA* 4. 232. 1-30.

every moment I water it lest anyone harm it. I protect it night and day, I have
no wrath. Who will give me thorns and briers." Behold, how he protects his Church
against any harm. For if he would let it be harmed, it could not possibly be protected. Harm would come to her if he would become angry and be the thorn in
the vineyard of the Church. His "protection" now refers to nothing other than
his personal appearance whereby he calms the terrified conscience.[48]

Further on Luther says that harm can come to the Church "only
when the devil succeeds to have that versatile sword, the Word of
God, which is more terrible to him than the whole of hell, cast away
and allowed to rust and decay."[49] The Church and the individual
faithful are therefore safe under God's rule.

1,9. "Thou hast loved justice and hated injustice; therefore God,
thy God, has anointed thee with the oil of gladness beyond thy com-
rades."

The thrust of Luther's discussion of 1, 9 becomes clear when one
sees it in the light of medieval exegesis. Luther's outburst against
"all the virtues of the philosophers, indeed of all men be they jurists
or theologians," and his attack on "the justice of man" make sense
when one realizes that some medieval exegetes define "justice" as
the sum and substance of virtue. Furthermore, there is a striking
difference between the way Luther and these medieval exegetes relate
1, 8 and 1, 9.

Chrysostom and Lyra interpret the verse in terms of what it says
about Christ's relationship to his Father. Alcuin and Aquinas interpret
the verse with reference to "virga"—Christ's love of justice shows
that his disciplining rod is just and fair. *Iustitia* for Alcuin and Aquinas
means *aequitas.*[50] The *Glossa interlinearis* and Tarantasia define justice
as "all good," and injustice as "all evil."[51] Dionysius the Carthusian
adds "virtue" to his definition of justice.[52]

Luther holds that the so-called virtues are really vices because
even if one is the best of virtuous men, he still loves himself more
than justice:

This text applies only to Christ because he alone loves justice, whereas all other
men love either money, pleasure, honor, glory, or themselves. If they despise
the first three they love at least glory. If they are the best kind of men, they love

---

[48] *WA* 57. III. 166. 18-26.

[49] *WA* 57. III. 169. 3-6.

[50] Alcuin, p. 1036; Aquinas, p. 349.

[51] *Glossa interlinearis*, f. 135r; Tarantasia, pp. 166-67.

[52] Dionysius the Carthusian, p. 475.

themselves more than justice.... While love of himself remains, man is utterly
unable to love, speak or do justice, even though he may be an accomplished hypo-
crite in all these things. It is a fact that all the virtues of the philosophers, indeed
of all men be they jurists or theologians, are virtues in appearance only but vices
in reality.[53]

The "justice of man" always remains basically selfish and covetous.
Luther thinks of justice in terms of "giving" (*reddo*). The "justice
of man" is never really justice because man only "renders to each
what is already his, namely, his money, possessions, honor or so on,
and does not give to others its own, but even covets the things of
others for itself." This is justice on a horizontal level. In the vertical
dimension "man in his justice never renders glory to God." Man by
himself thus is unable to be virtuous. Only Christ, who truly loves
justice, is able to bring about man's "love of justice." Justice in
this verse for Luther "stands for the justice of God and not for the
justice of man." God's justice is not selfish or covetous: "God in
his justice renders and gives himself and everything that is his to
God and to man." God's justice is his gift of justice to man:

> Therefore, it is only Christ who loves justice and hates injustice, whereas man
> loves injustice and hates justice. However, a Christian man begins to hate injustice
> and love justice, but he does so only through Christ, which is to say that Christ,
> the lover of justice, completes the beginning of our love by his own love.[54]

The clue then to verses 1, 8 and 1, 9 lies in Luther's opposition to
discipline and virtue which only bring about "vices in reality."
Luther's claim is that justice comes to man only through Christ
and his "staff," the gospel. The "staff" brings and effects justice—
God gives his justice through the gospel: "It is quite appropriate
that this text [1, 9] follows the phrase, 'a staff of guidance,' for the
'staff' itself effects this love of justice and hatred of injustice."[55]

D. By Way of Faith

2,10. "For it was fitting that he, for whom and by whom all things
exist, in bringing many sons to glory, should make the author of
their salvation perfect through suffering."

---

[53] *WA* 57. III. 110. 3-13.

[54] *WA* 57. III. 110. 14-24.

[55] *WA* 57. III. 110. 2-3.

A reading of Luther's exegesis of 2, 10 might lead one to the conclusion that Luther is only elaborating on traditional exegesis. For he cites and elaborates on the interpretations of Ambrose (perhaps a mistaken reference to Erasmus), Chrysostom and a "common saying."[56] However, one gains a different perspective of Luther's interpretation through a comparison with other medieval exegetes.

Chrysostom, Alcuin, and the *Glossa ordinaria* say that the phrase, "author of their salvation" demonstrates the distance and the gap between the Savior and the saved, whereas the phrase "who had brought many sons into glory" shows the opposite—that they are brought together in glory.[57] Luther explicitly draws upon Chrysostom for his interpretation but actually departs from the latter's exegesis. Luther holds that through Christ as "author" man is transformed (*conformari*) by faith into the very image of Christ. To Christ as *exemplar, signum* and *idea* man is conformed through faith:

> This verse beautifully shows how we are saved, namely, through Christ as archetype and example, to whose image all who are saved are conformed. For God the Father made Christ to be the sign and the archetype, so that those who adhere to him are transformed by faith into his image and thus drawn away from the images of the world.[58]

Christ as *auctor salutis* then brings God and man together in the present.

Later medieval exegetes interpret this verse in eschatological terms which only puts into sharper focus Luther's emphasis on the present. Aquinas, Lyra, and Dionysius the Carthusian employ futuristic terms— the inheritance of eternal life for those whom God has predestined. Aquinas says that God brings into glory those sons whom he predestined to bring. They become sons of God and heirs of eternal life through Christ as "author." Lyra says that Christ is "the author of the salvation of the elect." Dionysius the Carthusian says that God predestined from eternity those whom he would lead into glory and that Christ is the author of salvation for the elect—Christ earned salvation for the elect by his most worthy suffering.[59]

For Luther, the salvation of which Christ is "author" is available

---

[56] *WA* 57. III. 124. 4-9.

[57] Chrysostom, p. 265; Alcuin, p. 1041; *Glossa ordinaria*, f. 137v.

[58] *WA* 57. III. 124. 9-14.

[59] Aquinas, pp. 364-65; Lyra, f. 137v; Dionysius the Carthusian, p. 480.

to all through the gospel. God calls all men and draws them to himself through Christ who was exhibited to the whole world:

> This gathering of the sons of God unto one person is like the flocking together of the citizens when a magistrate calls a play: they leave their jobs and houses and pursue this one thing. It is exactly the same with Christ. Through the gospel, like a play exhibited to the whole world, he captivates all men in knowledge and contemplation of him and draws them away from that which binds them to the world.[60]

God takes the initiative in the salvation of man but not on the basis of predestination. Christ is "the most complete and absolute example" so as to attract men to adhere to him through faith.

In the light of medieval exegesis then the striking feature of Luther's interpretation is his contention that through Christ as *auctor salutis* the believer and Christ are united (*conformari*) in the present. Luther's idea of present conformity with the *auctor salutis* runs counter to Chrysostom, Alcuin, and the *Glossa ordinaria*. Luther's idea that such conformity is available to any and all believers runs counter to Aquinas, Lyra, and Dionysius the Carthusian.

Vogelsang and Boendermaker, who are interested in the concept of *conformitas* in the young Luther, depend heavily on Luther's exegesis of Heb. 2, 10 for their claim that *conformitas* with Christ is central to Luther's theology and that it refers to God's work in us. Vogelsang, who relies exclusively on Luther's exegesis of Heb. 2, 10, argues that *conformitas* means that Christ has identified himself with fallen man for us so that we might be identified with him through the work of Christ in us.[61]

Boendermaker relies mainly on Luther's exegesis of 2, 10 but also mentions that Luther twice quotes II Cor. 3, 18 where the word *transformari* is used and that *conformari* is also used in his Gloss on 13, 21.[62] Boendermaker discusses *conformitas* first in his chapter on "Some of the Important Theological Concepts in Luther's Lectures." He claims that the mystical overtones of *conformari* are very striking.[63] He argues that *conformitas* has to do with God's work in us and the relation between the Word and faith. Important for

---

[60] *WA* 57. III. 124. 16-125. 4.

[61] Vogelsang, *Die Bedeutung der neuveröffentlichten Hebräerbrief-Vorlesung Luthers,* p. 19.

[62] Boendermaker, *Luthers Commentaar op de Brief aan de Hebreeën,* p. 89.

[63] *Ibid.*

Boendermaker is the fact that *conformari* and *transformari* are used in the passive, which means that man is passive over against God, who is at work in man.[64]

In the light of medieval exegesis one gets a different picture of the meaning and significance of Luther's use of *conformari* and *transformari*. The emphasis of Luther here is not on God's initiative but rather on the fact that Christ and man come together through faith— the relationship is the important thing. This relationship of conformity is constituted in the present through faith and not consummated in the future on the basis of predestination.

E. Priest Without Comparison

5,1. "For every high priest chosen from among men is appointed to act for men in relation to God, to offer gifts and sacrifices for sins."

Luther's major concern in his exegesis of 5, 1 was discussed above— the significance of the phrase "for men" regarding the personal certitude of salvation. Another interest of Luther's is the Christological importance of the first part of the verse ("For every high priest chosen from among men").

Medieval exegetes from Chrysostom to Dionysius the Carthusian interpret the verse in terms of the relative superiority of the New Testament over the Old Testament. Christ as high priest is greater than any high priest in the Old Testament.

Chrysostom begins his interpretation of 5, 1 by saying that "St. Paul wishes to show now that this Testament is much better than the Old." Paul does so by showing first the similarities between the two Testaments and then the extent to which the New is superior. Comparatively speaking, Christ is superior to the high priests of the Old Testament. "Comparative excellence means that they share certain things in common and that in other matters he excels; otherwise it is not a matter of comparison."[65]

Alcuin and the *Glossa ordinaria* emphasize that because the New Testament is without a tangible temple, sacrificial animals and legal observances, it is "higher" and "more perfect" than the Old Testament.[66] Aquinas and Lyra outline the epistle so that, beginning with

---

[64] *Ibid.*, p. 121.

[65] Chrysostom, pp. 290-91.

[66] Alcuin, p. 1052; *Glossa ordinaria*, f. 141v.

chapter 5, Paul's intent is to demonstrate that Christ is *excellentior* than Aaron, the administrator of the law.[67] For Dionysius the Carthusian, Christ is of "superior excellence" compared with the priests of the Old Testament.[68]

For Luther there is no basis of comparison between the two Testaments. There is only stark contrast. In the light of medieval exegesis which was concerned to show the comparative superiority of Christ, Luther's use of the superlative hits one in the face. Christ is not a greater high priest but "the greatest high priest" who stands on a completely different level from Aaron. With reference to Aaron's carrying the sins of his people Luther says:

> This certainly prefigures that which was to take place, namely, that Christ, the greatest high priest, would bear the sins of all those who made offerings, that is, of those who believed.

Aaron is seen by Luther as a *praesignatum* of Christ. Christ is the point of reference and not Aaron or Moses. Both Aaron and Moses are interpreted by Luther to "prefigure" Christ:

> For Christ not only revealed sin as Moses did, but also like Aaron bore and took away sins. This is prefigured in Ps. 77, 20: "Thou didst lead the children of Israel by the hand of Moses and Aaron." They were led not only by the hand of Moses but even more so by the hand of Aaron, because "knowledge of sin" comes through Moses, that is, "through the law," which leads no one to life unless there be remission and cleansing of sin through Aaron, that is, through grace.[69]

5,6. "Thou art a priest forever, after the order of Melchisedec."

Luther's discussion of Christ in relation to Melchisedec is at first glance puzzling. Although medieval exegetes attach a great deal of importance to the Melchisedec passages, Luther selects only two of them (5, 6 and 7, 1) for a brief discussion of Melchisedec. There are ten Melchisedec passages in Hebrews: 5, 6-10; 6, 20; 7, 1, 10, 11, 15, 17, 21 and 28. The puzzle is solved when one realizes what importance Melchisedec had in medieval exegesis and that the significance of Luther's interpretation lies not in what he says but in what he does not say.

7, 1 is the best context in which to see the importance of Melchisedec in medieval exegesis. Chrysostom sets the stage for medieval exegesis

---

[67] Aquinas, p. 389; Lyra, f. 141v.

[68] Dionysius the Carthusian, p. 489.

[69] *WA* 57. III. 165. 15-166. 4.

of 7, 1. Paul's concern in chapter 7 for Chrysostom is to show the difference between the two Testaments. The fact that Christ is priest "after the order of Melchisedec" only substantiates Chrysostom's argument because Melchisedec was "more glorious" than the priests of the Old Testament and even greater than Abraham. Christ is the reality of which Melchisedec is the type. The name Melchisedec—king of righteousness—and the description of him as the king of Salem—king of peace—both refer to Christ who is the only king of righteousness and peace. Also, Paul's description of Melchisedec as "without beginning of days nor end of life" is meant to represent Christ, for the Old Testament is simply silent about Melchisedec's birth, death and genealogy. Melchisedec, who is the type of Christ, is superior to Abraham because Abraham paid a tithe to Melchisedec and was blessed by him. Thus the *excellentia* and superiority of Christ over the old dispensation is demonstrated by the fact that Christ is "after the order of Melchisedec" who was greater than the great forefather of the Old Testament and the subsequent priestly institutions.[70]

Aquinas, Tarantasia, Lyra and Dionysius the Carthusian follow Chrysostom's lead and interpret Melchisedec as the figure of Christ to be further proof of the *excellentia Christi*.[71] The point is that Melchisedec is superior to Aaron, father of the Levitical priesthood; thus Christ who is in reality what Melchisedec signified is superior to Aaron.

Luther's exegesis of 5, 6 is striking because of what he fails to say rather than because of what he does say. Luther's sole point, which is not unique, is that " 'After the order' means after the ordering, that is, after the history and deeds (*rem gestam*) of Melchisedec, whose deeds are narrated and recorded in Gen. 14."[72] Tarantasia also says that Melchisedec signifies Christ "through the history of deeds (*rei gestae*)" recorded in Genesis. In his discussion of 5, 6 then, Luther is not interested in the relative superiority of Christ over Aaron and the priests of the Old Testament, as were medieval exegetes.

In his exegesis of 7, 1, Luther again omits a discussion of the comparative excellence of Christ. He is concerned to show how absolutely different the way of Christ is from every aspect of the old way of

---

[70] Chrysostom, pp. 316-19.

[71] Aquinas, p. 407; Tarantasia, p. 206; Lyra, f. 144v-145r; Dionysius the Carthusian, p. 496.

[72] *WA* 57. III. 172. 4-16.

salvation, including the part of Melchisedec. Luther concentrates not
on the relative superiority of Melchisedec over Abraham and Aaron
but simply on the soteriological importance of Christ as king of
righteousness and peace:

> "Melech" in Hebrew means king, just as "salem" means peace and "sedek" righ-
> teousness. We should note, however, that in holy Scripture this "righteousness"
> and "peace" always refer to God's righteousness and God's peace. Thus "righteous-
> ness" is that very grace itself by which man is justified, that is, faith, hope, and
> love.... Thus it follows that this Melchisedec cannot possibly be "the king of
> righteousness" unless he represents Christ in name and figure. Christ alone is
> "the son of righteousness" and "the king of righteousness," justifying all the
> just. Therefore, we have to take off our shoes, that is, get rid of the illusion that
> human righteousness can be acquired by one's own acts.[73]

Luther addresses himself to the question of "the excellence of
Christ and his priesthood," but the upshot of his argument is that
Christ is not relatively superior but absolutely superior because he
is not only different from Aaron and Abraham but also different
from Melchisedec:

> The apostle indicates four elements which constitute the excellence of Christ and
> his priesthood: eternity, blessing, everlasting duration and tithing. Eternity insofar
> as Christ is prefigured through Melchisedec, for whom no birth is recorded. Blessing
> insofar as Abraham was blessed by Melchisedec and through this all the sons of
> Abraham, with the exception of Christ. Tithing insofar as Abraham and Levi
> gave tithes to Melchisedec as the more worthy, but not so Christ. Everlasting
> duration insofar as Abraham and Levi died, but Christ lives forever. And so there
> is no place for the empty confidence of the Jews in their law and priesthood, since
> both they and their patriarchs are inferior to the one who blessed them.[74]

Luther is concerned to show that Christ is an exception even to
Melchisedec. The excellence of Christ stems from the absolute antithesis between the two testaments. Luther then, does not only treat
Melchisedec as proof for the comparative superiority of Christ but
views Melchisedec as proof of the radical uniqueness of Christ in
relation even to Melchisedec.

F. The Testament of Forgiveness

9,17. "For a testament takes effect only at death, since it is not
in force as long as the one who made it is alive."

---

[73] *WA* 57. III. 187. 4-188. 7.
[74] *WA* 57. III. 188. 18-30.

In his exegesis of 9, 17, Luther declares that he intends to "follow Chrysostom who makes use of the idea of a testament as implied in both Testaments."[75] However, he departs from Chrysostom on two accounts. In the first case he does so explicitly, but in the second his departure comes to light only through a comparison with the medieval exegetical tradition.

Chrysostom describes the characteristics of any testament—it is made towards the end of one's life, it makes some heirs and disinherits others, it contains certain commitments on the part of the testator and the legatees and, finally, it ought to have witnesses. Luther criticizes Chrysostom for failing to discuss the question of what Christ bequeathed in his testament—"This especially calls for discussion." Some medieval exegetes answer this question, and Luther's answer to this question is striking because of the difference between the answers.

Christ's last testament, according to the *Glossa interlinearis* is "the promise of eternal life and the teaching of the gospel."[76] This definition of the content of the new testament is repeated by Dionysius the Carthusian.[77] Other medieval exegetes in their interpretation of 9, 17 discuss the character and nature of a testament as Chrysostom did without discussing the actual content of Christ's testament.[78]

Medieval exegetes do discuss the content of the new testament in the context of 8, 6 ("Christ has obtained a ministry which is as much more excellent than the old as the covenant he mediates is better, since it is enacted on better promises"). They generally understand the content of the new testament to be the promise of eternal life, as does Luther in his Gloss on 8, 6.[79] Chrysostom says that the new testament is better because "instead of a temple, we have heaven."[80] The *Glossa interlinearis* says that the new testament is "better" "because it promises things eternal."[81] Aquinas and Lyra make the same claim.[82] Pseudo-Hugh of St. Victor says that the new testament

---

[75] *WA* 57. III. 211. 22-27.

[76] *Glossa interlinearis*, f. 151r.

[77] Dionysius the Carthusian, p. 507.

[78] *Glossa ordinaria*, f. 151r; Aquinas, p. 436; Lyra, f. 151r; Faber Stapulensis, f. 248v.

[79] *WA* 57. III. 45. 1.

[80] Chrysostom, p. 331.

[81] *Glossa interlinearis*, f. 148r.

[82] Aquinas, pp. 421-23; Lyra, f. 148r.

"contains the promise of an eternal inheritance."[83] Faber Stapulensis distinguishes between the two testaments by saying that the new testament is the promise of eternal life distinguished from the old which offers only temporal life.[84] Lyra succinctly states this medieval view in his exegesis of 7, 22. The new testament of Christ properly speaking "promises celestial and eternal *bona*."[85]

Against this medieval background of understanding the new testament as the promise of eternal life, Luther's interpretation of 9, 17 is strikingly different. Luther claims that in his testament Christ bequeathed an invaluable inheritance—"the forgiveness of sins and eternal life." In his discussion Luther accents the importance of understanding Christ's testament as the promise of the forgiveness of sins:

> But Chrysostom only briefly touches on what is to be received through the testament. This especially calls for discussion. It should be known, therefore, that an invaluable inheritance was willed and bequeathed in his most faithful testament— the forgiveness of sins and eternal life.[86]

Luther comes to his conclusion by arguing that the content of Christ's testament is contained in the words of institution at the Last Supper:

> Chrysostom bypasses the known fact that Christ made his testament "during the last days of his life." The Gospel accounts all agree that at the Last Supper when Christ had taken the cup and blessed it he said: "This is the new testament in my blood."[87]

Luther cites the Synoptics' account of the Last Supper to show that Christ shed his blood for the forgiveness of sins.[88] With reference to 9, 14, Luther says:

> No law, nor work, in fact nothing at all can effect this purity, except the blood of Christ alone, and not even Christ's blood unless man in his heart believes that it was poured out for the forgiveness of sins. Thus one must believe him who made the testament: "This is my blood which is poured out for you and for many for the forgiveness of sins" (Matt. 26, 28).[89]

---

[83] Ps.-Hugh of St. Victor, pp. 626-27.

[84] Faber Stapulensis, f. 246v.

[85] Lyra, f. 146v.

[86] *WA* 57. III. 212. 4-7.

[87] *WA* 57. III. 211. 28-212. 4.

[88] *WA* 57. III. 212. 8-12.

[89] *WA* 57. III. 207. 26-208. 4.

The significance of Luther's argument and his second departure from medieval exegesis is that he understands the sacrament of the altar to be a testament—the promise of the forgiveness of sins and eternal life. Luther's second departure then is related to the first and shows its importance.

Medieval exegetes do not discuss the Lord's Supper in connection with 9, 17 and the concept of testament as does Luther but rather in connection with 10, 1-3 and the concept of sacrifice. 10, 1-3:

> For since the law has but a shadow of the good things to come instead of the true form of these realities, it can never, by the same sacrifices which are continually offered year after year, make perfect those who draw near. Otherwise, would they not have ceased to be offered? If the worshippers had once been cleansed, they would no longer have any consciousness of sin. But in these sacrifices there is a reminder of sin year after year.

For Chrysostom the Eucharist is a sacrifice. Though Christ is offered many times in many different places the sacrifice is always the same:

> For just aι ᴜe who is offered everywhere is one body and not many, so also there is one sacrifice. He is our high priest who offered the sacrifice that cleanses us. We offer now that which was offered then; which is inconsumable.... We do not offer a different sacrifice as the high priest did, but always the same; or rather, we celebrate a memorial of a sacrifice.[90]

Other medieval exegetes are concerned to stress that the sacrifice of the Eucharist is not a new or different sacrifice other than that offered by Christ on the cross. The *Glossa ordinaria* says that "what we offer daily is a memorial (*recordatio*) of his death." The sacrifice of Christ in the Eucharist wherever offered is the same but never consumed.[91] Aquinas says that the Eucharist is an offer of nothing other than what Christ offered for us—his blood. "It is not a different sacrifice but a *commemoratio* of the sacrifice which Christ offered."[92] Comparing the two Testaments in his exegesis of 7, 12, Aquinas holds that the sacraments of the new law confer grace *ex opere operato*.[93] Lyra holds that Christ's sacrifice can never be repeated. The Eucharist is a *commemoratio* of his offer—"the same is offered that he offered."[94]

---

[90] Chrysostom, p. 349.
[91] *Glossa ordinaria*, f. 152r.
[92] Aquinas, p. 442.
[93] Aquinas, p. 414.
[94] Lyra, f. 152r.

Lyra also says that the sacrifices of the old law were acceptable to God *ex fide* and not *ex re ipsa* as are the sacrifices of the new law.[95]

Regarding 10, 1-3, Chrysostom, the *Glossa ordinaria*, Aquinas and Lyra discuss the Eucharist in terms of a sacrifice and a memorial—a memorial of Christ's sacrifice. Aquinas and Lyra say that the fruit or purpose of the Eucharist is conveyed *ex opere operato* to the recipient.

Luther does not have a Scholium on 10, 1-3 and in his Gloss on 10, 1-3 he does not mention the Lord's Supper. Luther does quote from Chrysostom's exegesis of 10, 1-3 in his interpretation of 9, 24. He does so, however, to de-emphasize the sacrificial character of the Eucharist:

> Why don't we stop our offering now, since we are perfect and righteous through the grace of baptism and repentance? For Christ is offered daily on our behalf. Chrysostom responds: "We offer indeed for the remembrance of his death, and this is the one sacrifice which was offered once and for all." I interpret this to mean that Christ was offered once only, as said in the preceding chapter. What now is offered by us every day is not so much offer as memorial of his offer, as he said: "Do this in remembrance of me" (I Cor. 11, 24).[96]

Luther selects his quotation from Chrysostom to emphasize the memorial character of the Eucharist over against its sacrificial character. His quotation presents a one-sided view of Chrysostom who had also said, "We offer that now which was offered then." For Luther the Eucharist is not the continual offer of Christ but rather the continual offer of the body of Christ, the Church:

> Therefore, this offering of the new testament as far as Christ, the head of the Church, is concerned, is complete and finished. However, the spiritual offer of his body, which is the Church, is offered from day to day, whereby we continually die with Christ and mystically celebrate his passover.[97]

Throughout his *Lectures on Hebrews* Luther uses the concept of the Eucharist as a testament rather than a sacrifice. This is not to say that testament and sacrifice are mutually exclusive categories.[98] It is rather that Luther's discussion of the Eucharist in terms of a

---

[95] Lyra, f. 154r.

[96] *WA* 57. III. 217. 25-218. 2.

[97] *WA* 57. III. 218. 5-8.

[98] Regin Prenter, "Luther on Word and Sacrament," *More About Luther* ("Martin Luther Lectures," Vol. 2; Decorah, Iowa, 1958), pp. 112-18.

testament leads him to different conclusions from those of medieval exegetes who discuss it in terms of a sacrifice.

For Luther the Eucharist as a testament is a promise of the forgiveness of sins. The promise requires the response and acceptance of faith. In the context of 5, 1 and 7, 12 Luther opposes the *obex* doctrine of Lombard and others—namely, that the Eucharist conveys grace efficaciously to all who do not put up an obstacle (*obex*).[99] The Eucharist requires more than the absence of mortal sin, more than confession and preparations: "Any sacrament requires a most pure heart, otherwise man shall be guilty of the sacrament and receive his judgment. However, the heart can only be purified through faith."[100] Those who do not come in faith "eat and drink judgment unto themselves."[101]

We see as a result of Luther's exegesis of 5, 1 that he holds to the real presence of Christ at the altar and does not depart from Aquinas and Lyra on this score. Elsewhere Luther reinforces this idea. Regarding 9, 2 he says that in the sacrament we receive and eat (*pascimur*) Christ, and that "Christ comes to us daily in the sacrament."[102] In the context of 9, 4, Luther says that the external Word and sacrament are common (*communia*) to both the worthy and unworthy.[103]

Luther does depart from Aquinas and Lyra regarding the efficacy of the Eucharist. And that is because he regards the words of institution to be a promise which is efficacious for salvation only to those who believe. Luther states his position succinctly in his exegesis of 7, 12:

> Therefore, the apostle describes Christ as "one who pledges a better covenant" (Heb. 7, 22), because he promises the forgiveness of sins and purity of heart through the Word of his priest, so that all who believe this Word are completely righteous and pure before God.[104]

The significance of Luther's exegesis of 9, 17, therefore, has to do with his understanding of testament. In the light of medieval exegesis two aspects of his interpretation stand out. The first is that the

---

[99] *WA* 57. III. 170. 7; 191. 22.
[100] *WA* 57. III. 170. 8-10.
[101] *WA* 57. III. 171. 1.
[102] *WA* 57. III. 200. 3-4.
[103] *WA* 57. III. 200. 19-20.
[104] *WA* 57. III. 192. 12-15.

testament of Christ is the promise of the forgiveness of sins as well
as eternal life. The second is that the Eucharist is a testament which
requires faith for salubrious efficacy.

G. SACRAMENTUM ET EXEMPLUM

10,19. "Therefore, brethren, since we have confidence to enter the
sanctuary by the blood of Jesus..."

In his exegesis of 10, 19, Luther deals with the work of Christ in
terms of "sacramentum" and "exemplum." Luther begins his interpretation by saying that "the apostle wants us to imitate Christ, who
suffered and by dying passed over to the glory of the Father."[105]
The passion and resurrection of Christ is "the sacrament for imitating
Christ"—a sacrament "for the mortification of concupiscence" and
"for our new life." Luther then says, "almost all of Paul's epistles are
full of this mystical and exemplary suffering of Christ."[106]

The passion of Christ is "exemplary" in a twofold way. Referring
to St. Augustine[107] Luther says:

> We pass over in flesh and spirit, but Christ in flesh alone. Therefore, the passing
> over of Christ's flesh is at the same time an example for the passing over of our
> flesh (for we will be like him), and a sacrament for the passing over of our spirit.[108]

The reference to Augustine, made here and in the lectures on Romans
and Galatians,[109] show that the sacrament of Christ's passion and
resurrection is the work of Christ for man's salvation. Man is called
to imitate Christ's sacrament by dying to sin and walking a new way
with Christ. Christ's death and resurrection is also an example for
man to die physically in order to be reunited with Christ in heaven.[110]

In the light of medieval exegesis the conclusion which Luther draws
from his discussion of *sacramentum* and *exemplum* is striking: because
of the *sacramentum* and *exemplum* of Christ "we have confidence to
enter the sanctuary by the blood of Jesus" (10, 19).

---

[105] *WA* 57. III. 222. 12-14.

[106] *WA* 57. III. 222. 23-223. 5.

[107] *De trinitate* IV. 3. 5-6.

[108] *WA* 57. III. 223. 11-14.

[109] *WA* 56. 320. 11 ff., 57. II. 54. 4-9.

[110] Erwin Iserloh, "Sacramentum et exemplum: ein augustinisches Thema lutherischer Theologie," *Reformata Reformanda: Festgabe für Hubert Jedin zum 17. Juni
1965*, ed. Erwin Iserloh and Konrad Repgen (Münster i. W., 1965), I, 257-58.

Chrysostom and the *Glossa ordinaria* argue that "we have confidence" because the realities of the New Testament are greater than the types of the Old Testament.[111] The *Glossa interlinearis* emphasizes that our certainty comes from the fact that Christ was the first "to enter."[112] Tarantasia says that Christ is an infallible *dux*.[113] Dionysius the Carthusian says that Christ "prepared and demonstrated," "opened" and "initiated" the way for us "to enter."[114]

For Luther the example of Christ is that he "passed over before everyone else and levelled the rough road in order to elicit our confidence." However, Christ does more than show us the way, "he also holds out his hand for those who are following." Our confidence rests in the fact that "Christ alone is not only our companion on the way, but also our leader (*dux*), and not only leader but also helper, in fact he carries us over."[115] Christ as example, therefore, shows us how to die confidently. Christ as sacrament made it possible for us to die confidently, and he continues to do so.

In the light of medieval exegesis the significance of Luther's interpretation of 10, 19 is that "we have confidence to enter the sanctuary" not because Christ's testament is greater than the Old but because of Christ alone—his sacrament and example. Furthermore our confidence arises from the fact that Christ not only opened the way but also carries us over.

H. Conclusion

In this chapter we have seen that for Luther the only way to God is by way of faith in the lowly humanity of Christ, the holy ladder of ascent to God, who became the most abject of men for man in his passion and death. His strong soteriological emphasis in his exegesis of Hebrews provokes him to ignore the Trinitarian interests so persistent in his medieval predecessors. He concentrates rather on the fact that man's righteousness is effected by Christ's own righteousness, and his penance by Christ's purgation. It is Christ who

---

[111] Chrysostom, p. 357.

[112] *Glossa interlinearis*, f. 153r.

[113] Tarantasia, p. 240.

[114] Dionysius the Carthusian, p. 511.

[115] *WA* 57. III. 223. 24-224. 10.

accomplishes salvation in man, rather than the inadequate human efforts to achieve forgiveness.

Viewing Christ in this manner, it follows for Luther to see the people of God, the Church, as a royal people presently existing under the contradiction of the cross. In such an exile they are protected and made new only by the "staff" of God, the power of his Word. By their faith these people are captivated by Christ, their priest without example, and are in the present related to him through conformity to him. Their faith rests in his testament to them—the promise of the forgiveness of sins. Their confidence is made certain because of the *sacramentum* and *exemplum* of Christ's passion and resurrection. The removed Trinitarian God of justice and discipline delineated by the medieval exegetes gives way in Luther's exegesis to the "worm" who brings to man, through his "staff," God's power for salvation, the gift of God's righteousness, and who carries his people to the Father.

CONCLUSION

The development of Christian thought as the development of biblical exegesis has been the perspective of this study in order to assess what the students in Wittenberg in 1517 were hearing from their increasingly popular Professor of Bible. While the academic and liturgical traditions are important for the context of Luther's *Lectures on Hebrews*, this study singled out the exegetical tradition as a base and frame of reference with which to examine Luther's theology in his interpretation of Hebrews. This exegetical tradition has been seen to be very important for the understanding of Luther's lectures because, far more than his own references indicate, Luther is very much in dialog with his medieval predecessors in their various interpretations of Hebrews.

The story of how Luther's lectures were received, first by his students and later by his modern interpretors, has been traced. Boendermaker did the first and only analysis of the *Lectures on Hebrews* in the light of medieval exegesis. His study has been seen to be insufficient. Other earlier studies of these lectures were basically summaries of their contents. They did little to explain Luther's thought in relation to his background or his own previous work. What more adequately constitutes the medieval exegetical tradition includes those exegetes of Hebrews whom Luther definitely used, those he probably was aware of, and those who were important in the development of exegesis.

Luther's considerable exegetical productivity, competent as it was by contemporary Humanistic standards, was aimed at reuniting theology and exegesis. The exegetical theology that emerges in his *Lectures on Hebrews* revolves around the category of *testamentum* and concerns the problem of authorship, the relationship between the two testaments, faith, and Christology.

In the brief introduction to his lectures, Luther accepts Pauline authorship of Hebrews without discussion. In the light of traditional exegesis, the striking aspect about Luther's introduction is that he does not discuss the authorship, whereas medieval exegetes did so rather extensively. Throughout the lectures, Luther sees no significant occasion to change his mind about the authorship of Hebrews, yet he does raise questions and, in a few places, expresses doubts about

Pauline authorship. In contrast to his predecessors, such problems as the relation of Heb. 2, 3 to Gal. 1, the language of 2, 10, and the questionable references in Hebrews to the Old Testament (that is, the problem of the two Testaments), are seen by Luther to involve the authorship question.

The most striking aspect about Luther's introduction is its statement of the basic content of the Epistle: the relationship of Christ to the Old Testament. In order to gain a fuller appreciation of medieval discussion of the relationship between the two Testaments, a rather nuanced study of *testamentum* in Augustine was undertaken. We concluded that there are various aspects to Augustine's theology of testament. There is a discussion of how the two eras fit into the divine plan of salvation (providential categories) and a discussion of the congruence of the two books (hermeneutical categories). The two testaments for Augustine, also represent two types of men, *animalia* and *spiritualia*, and the difference is a matter of "growing up" in the faith.

Medieval exegetes generally hold that the New Testament is more excellent than the Old, and the problem is approached in hermeneutical and providential terms. Luther emphasizes the "antithesis" rather than the comparison, contrast and development between them, and he approaches the problem in soteriological terms. The antithesis is continuous and dialectical. It is not one of two different time periods, but one of two different, and continuously different, types of response to the one Word, testament, of God: *simul vetus et novum testamentum*. By Anselmian standards this does not adequately explain, "cur Deus homo?" Yet for Luther, *theologia crucis* means *theologia testamenti*—the cross is assumed and not argued. The old and new types of response are possible for Luther during the time of the Old and New Testaments precisely because Christ makes all the difference—the *testamentum Christi* is the Word of the Lord to his royal people.

Methodologically, the chapter on testament raised the question of Luther's theology of testament precisely by examining his *Lectures on Hebrews* in the light of medieval exegesis. It would seem indispensable for any future work on Luther's early exegesis to employ this method, and a study of "Augustine and..." is always relevant. Also methodologically important, this chapter examined the *Dictata* with an eye to those Psalm verses which Luther cited in his *Lectures on Hebrews* in order to compare Luther's thought associated with these psalms over a five year period. With minor exegetical exceptions, no significant change was seen in Luther's thought.

In the chapters on Faith and Christology—two prominent themes in the *Lectures on Hebrews*—the method of examining these lectures in the light of medieval exegesis and Luther's own previous exegesis was continued.

Faith for Luther is the difference between the testaments. One who "hears" the eternal testament possesses the promised eternal goods. What for medieval exegetes pertains to the future and the realm of *fides formata caritate*, for Luther involves the present and the certitude of salvation. Faith for Luther is the first and last response of man to God's testament, whereas for medieval exegetes faith is only the first of several necessary steps for the completion of one's future salvation.

Present and personal certitude of salvation is possible in Luther's theology because of the *testamentum Christi*. In addition to the promise of eternal life, the sole emphasis of medieval exegetes, Luther considers the importance of Christ's testament to be the forgiveness of sins. The sacrament and example of Christ's death gives assurance that Christ, the "Träger," is not only the testator but also the one who effects forgiveness of sins. Rather than discuss the Eucharist in the context of "sacrifice texts," as the medieval exegetes do, Luther discusses the sacrament of the testament of Christ in terms of the forgiveness of sins and the response of faith made possible by Christ.

We have seen that the category of testament, as developed in some medieval theology has opened up some new possibilities for our understanding of the young Luther. The next step would be to see what happens historically to this young Luther's *theologia testamenti*.

BIBLIOGRAPHY

Primary Sources

Alcuin, *Expositio in epistolam Pauli apostoli ad Hebraeos*. *PL* 100 (Paris, 1863) 1031-84.

Aquinas, St. Thomas, "Super epistolam ad Hebraeos lectura," *Super epistolas sancti Pauli lectura*. Ed. P. Raphaelis Cai, O.P. Vol. 2, 8th ed. (Rome, 1953) 335-506.

Augustine, *De moribus ecclesiae catholicae* (388). *PL* 32 (Paris, 1877) 1310-1334.

——, *De vera religione* (390). *CCSL* 32 (Turnholti, 1962) 169-260.

——, *De utilitate credendi* (392). *CSEL* 25 (Vienna, 1891) 1-48.

——, *Ennarationes in Psalmos* (392-418). *CCSL* 38-40 (Turnholti, 1956).

——, *Contra Adimantum* (ca. 394). *CSEL* 25 (Vienna, 1891) 115-90.

——, *Contra Faustum* (398). *CSEL* 25 (Vienna, 1891) 249-797.

——, *De catechizandis rudibus* (ca. 399). *CCSL* 46 (Turnholti, 1969) 115-78.

——, *De baptismo contra Donatistas* (400). *CSEL* 51 (Vienna, 1908) 143-375.

——, *Ad Honoratum* (412). *CSEL* 44 (Vienna, 1904).

——, *De civitate dei* (ca. 413-427). *CCSL* 47-48 (Turnholti, 1955).

——, *Quaestiones in Heptateuchum* (419-420). *CCSL* 33 (Turnholti, 1958) 1-377.

——, *Contra adversarium legis et prophetarum* (420). *PL* 42 (Paris, 1886) 605-66.

——, *Contra duas epistulas Pelagianorum* (ad Bonafacium) (n.d.). *CSEL* 60 (Vienna, 1913) 421-570.

Biblia cum Glossa ordinaria, Nicolai de Lyra postilla, moralitatibus eiusdem, Pauli Burgensis additionibus, Matthiae Thoring replicis. 6 Vols. (Basel, 1506-08).

Biblia ... cum concordantiis ... summariis omnium capitum, divisionibus, quattuor repertoriis propositis ... una cum vera nominum Hebraicorum interpretatione (Basel, 1509).

Biblia cum concordantiis veteris et novi testamenti necnon et iuris canonici, ac diversitatibus textuum, canonibusque evangeliorum ac quibusdam temporum incidentibus in margine positis et accentu singularum dictionum (Venice, 1511).

Burgos, Paul, Cf. *Biblia cum Glossa* ...

Chrysostom, St. John, *Homilae XXXIV in epistolam ad Hebraeos*. *PG* 63 (Paris, 1862) 237-456.

Dionysius the Carthusian, "Enarratio in epistolam beati Pauli ad Hebraeos," *Enarrationes piae ac eruditae in beati Pauli epistolas*. "Omnia Opera," Vol. 13 (Monstrolius, 1901) 469-531.

Doering, Matthias, Cf. *Biblia cum Glossa* ...

Erasmus, Desiderius, *Novum instrumentum cum Annotationibus* (Basel, 1516).

Ps.-Hugh of St. Victor, "In epistolam ad Hebraeos," *Quaestiones et decisiones in epistolas divi Pauli*. *PL* 175 (Paris, 1879) 607-34.

Luther, Martin, "Lectures on the Epistle to the Hebrews 1517-18," *Luther: Early Theological Works*. Ed. James Atkinson. "The Library of Christian Classics," Vol. 16 (Philadelphia, 1962) 19-250.

——, "Lectures on Hebrews," *Lectures on Titus, Philemon and Hebrews*. Ed. Jaroslav Pelikan. *LW* 29 (St. Louis, 1968) 109-241.

——, *Luthers Hebräerbrief-Vorlesung von 1517-18. Deutsche Übersetzung*. Ed. Erich Vogelsang. "Arbeiten zur Kirchengeschichte," Vol. 17 (Berlin, 1930).

——, *Luthers Vorlesung über den Hebräerbrief nach der Vatikanischen Handschrift.* Ed. Emanuel Hirsch and Hanns Rückert. "Arbeiten zur Kirchengeschichte," Vol. 13 (Berlin, 1929).

——, *Luthers Vorlesung über den Hebräerbrief 1517-18.* Ed. Johannes Ficker. "Anfänge reformatorischer Bibelauslegung," Vol. 2 (Leipzig, 1929).

——, *Martin Luther. Vorlesung über den Hebräerbrief 1517-18.* Ed. Georg Helbig (Leipzig, 1930).

——, *Martin Luthers Werke, Kritische Gesammtausgabe.* Especially Vols. 3, 4, 55. I and II, 56, 57 (Weimar, 1883 ff.).

Petrus de Tarantasia, "In epistolam b. Pauli ad Hebraeos," *In omnes divi Pauli epistolas enarratio.* Ed. Nicolas de Gorran, O.P., Vol. 2 (Lyon, 1692) 160-282.

Stapulensis, Jacobus Faber, *Epistolae Pauli apostoli.* 1st ed. (Paris, 1512).

Valla, Lorenzo, *Adnotationes in latinam Novi Testamenti interpretationem.* Ed. Erasmus (Paris, 1505).

Secondary Sources

Barth, Peter, "Luther zum Hebräerbrief," *Die Christliche Welt* 44 (1930) 954-58.

Baruzi, Jean, "Le commentaire de Luther à l'Épître aux Hebreux," *Revue d'Histoire, et de Philosophie Religieuses* 11 (1931) 461-98.

Bayer, Oswald, *Promissio. Geschichte der reformatorischen Wende in Luthers Theologie* "Forschungen zur Kirchen und Dogmengeschichte," Vol. 24 (Göttingen, 1971).

Bizer, Ernst, *Fides ex Auditu. Eine Untersuchung über die Entdeckung der Gerechtigkeit Gottes durch Martin Luther.* 3rd ed. (Darmstadt, 1966).

Böhmer, Heinrich, *Der junge Luther.* Ed. Heinrich Bornkamm (Stuttgart, 1951).

Boendermaker, J.P., *Luthers Commentaar op de Brief aan de Hebreeën 1517-1518* (Assen, 1965).

Brandenburg, Albert, " 'Solae aures sunt organa Christiani hominis.' Zu Luthers Exegese von Hebr. 10, 5 f." *Einsicht und Glaube. Gottlieb Sohngen zum 70. Geburtstag.* Ed. Joseph Ratzinger and Heinrich Fries (Freiburg, 1962).

Camp P. Ulfridus van, O.F.M., *De habitudine missae ad sacrificium crucis apud commentatores latinos epistolae ad Hebraeos usque ad Petrum Lombardum.* "Pontificium Athenaeum Antonianum Facultas Theologica. Theses ad Lauream N. 151" (Katanga, 1962).

Concordantiae Augustinianae sive collectio omnium sententiarum quae sparsim reperiuntur in omnibus S. Augustini operibus. Ed. F. David Lenfant. 2 Vols. (Paris, 1656-65).

Denifle, Heinrich, O.P., *Die abendländischen Schriftausleger bis Luther über "Justitia Dei" (Rom. 1, 17) und "Justificatio."* Vol. 1, Part 2, 2nd ed. (Mainz, 1905).

Ebeling, Gerhard, *Evangelische Evangelienauslegung. Eine Untersuchung zu Luthers Hermeneutik.* (Munich, 1942).

——, "Die Anfänge von Luthers Hermeneutik," *Zeitschrift für Theologie und Kirche* 48 (1951) 172-230.

Ellwein, Eduard, "Zu Luthers Hebräerbriefvorlesung," *Zwischen den Zeiten* 9 (1931) 547-49.

——, "Die Entfaltung der theologia crucis in Luthers Hebräerbrief-vorlesung," *Theologische Aufsätze: Karl Barth, zum 50. Geburtstag* (Munich, 1936) 382-404.

Feld, Helmut, *Martin Luthers und Wendelin Steinbachs Vorlesungen über den Hebräer-brief. Eine Studie zur Geschichte der neutestamentlichen Exegese und Theologie.* "Veröffentlichungen des Institutes für europäische Geschichte Mainz," Vol. 62 (Wiesbaden, 1971).

Greschat, Martin, "Der Bundesgedanke in der Theologie des späten Mittelalters,'ₜ *Zeitschrift für Kirchengeschichte* 81 (1970) 44-63.

Gyllenkrok, Axel, *Rechtfertigung und Heiligung in der frühen evangelischen Theologie Luthers* (Uppsala, 1952).

Hagen, Kenneth, "The First Translation of Luther's *Lectures on Hebrews*: A Review Article," *Church History* 34 (1965) 204-13.

——, "Changes in the Understanding of Luther: The Development of the Young Luther," *Theological Studies* 29 (1968) 472-96.

——, "An Addition to the Letters of John Lang: Introduction and Translation," *Archiv für Reformationsgeschichte* 60/1 (1969) 27-32.

——, "From Testament to Covenant in the Early Sixteenth Century," *The Sixteenth Century Journal* 3 (April, 1972) 1-24.

Hailperin, Herman, *Rashi and the Christian Scholars* (Pittsburgh, 1963).

Hamel, Adolf, *Der junge Luther und Augustin, ihre Beziehungen in der Rechtfertigungs-lehre nach Luthers ersten Vorlesungen 1509-18.* 2 Vols. (Gütersloh, 1934-35).

Holl, Karl, *Gesammelte Aufsätze zur Kirchengeschichte 1: Luther.* 6th ed. (Tübingen, 1932).

Iserloh, Erwin, "Sacramentum et exemplum: ein augustinisches Thema lutherischer Theologie," *Reformata Reformanda: Festgabe für Hubert Jedin zum 17. Juni 1965.* Ed. Erwin Iserloh and Konrad Repgen. Vol. I (Münster i. W., 1965) 247-64

Jørgensen, Alfred, "Luthers Forelaesning over Hebraeerbrevet," *For laere og liv. Fests-krift til Det teologiske Menighetsfakultets 25års jubilaeum* (Oslo, 1933) 176-204.

Landgraf, A., "Familienbildung bei Paulinenkommentaren des 12. Jahrhunderts," *Biblica* 13 (1932) 61-72, 169-93.

——, "Untersuchung zu den Paulinenkommentaren des 12. Jahrhunderts," *Recherches de Théologie Ancienne et Médiévale* 8 (1936) 253-81.

Lubac, Henri de, "A propos de la formule: Diversi sed non adversi," *Recherches de Science Religieuse* 40 (1952) 27-40.

——, *The Sources of Revelation.* Tr. Luke O'Neill (New York, 1968).

Lortz, Joseph, *Die Reformation in Deutschland.* 4th Ed. (Freiburg, 1962).

Müller, Alphons Victor, "Luthers Lehre in ihrem Verhältnis zu Augustin und zur augustinischen Tradition," *Luther in ökumenischer Sicht.* Ed. Alfred von Martin (Stuttgart, 1929) 38-64.

Oberman, Heiko A., " 'Facientibus quod in se est Deus non denegat gratiam.' Robert Holcot, O.P., and the Beginnings of Luther's Theology," *Harvard Theological Review* 55 (1962) 317-342.

——, *The Harvest of Medieval Theology. Gabriel Biel and Late Medieval Nominalism* (Cambridge, 1963).

——, " 'Iustitia Christi' and 'Iustitia Dei': Luther and the Scholastic Doctrines of Justification," *Harvard Theological Review* 59 (1966) 1-26.

——, " 'Simul Gemitus et Raptus': Luther und die Mystik," *The Church, Mysticism, Sanctification and the Natural in Luther's Thought.* Ed. Ivar Asheim (Philadelphia, 1967) 20-59.

——, "Wir sein pettler. Hoc est verum. Bund und Gnade in der Theologie des Mittel-alters und der Reformation," *Zeitschrift für Kirchengeschichte* 78 (1967) 232-52.

Ozment, Steven E., *Homo Spiritualis. A Comparative Study of the Anthropology of Johannes Tauler, Jean Gerson and Martin Luther (1509-1516) in the Context of their Theological Thought.* "Studies in Medieval and Reformation Thought," Vol. 6 (Leiden, 1969).

Pesch, Otto H., O.P., *Theologie der Rechtfertigung bei Martin Luther und Thomas von Aquin: Versuch eines systematisch-theologischen Dialogs* (Mainz, 1967).

Pilch, John, "Luther's Hermeneutical Shift," *Harvard Theological Review* 60 (1970) 445-48.

Pontet, Maurice, *L'Exégèse de S. Augustin Prédicateur* (Paris, 1944).

Prenter, Regin, "Luther on Word and Sacrament," *More About Luther.* "Martin Luther Lectures," Vol. 2 (Decorah, Iowa, 1958) 65-122.

Preus, James Samuel, *From Shadow to Promise. Old Testament Interpretation from Augustine to the Young Luther* (Cambridge, 1969).

Riggenbach, Eduard, *Historische Studien zum Hebräerbrief.* Part I: *Die ältesten lateinischen Kommentare zum Hebräerbrief.* "Forschungen zur Geschichte des neutestamentlichen Kanons und der altkirchlichen Literatur" (Leipzig, 1907).

Scheel, Otto, "Die Textausgaben der Vorlesung Luthers über den Hebräerbrief," *Theologische Studien und Kritiken* 102 (1930) 202-10.

Schwarz, Reinhard, *Fides, spes und charitas beim jungen Luther, unter besonderer Berücksichtigung der mittelalterlichen Tradition.* "Arbeiten zur Kirchengeschichte," Vol. 34 (Berlin, 1962).

Smalley, Beryl, *The Study of the Bible in the Middle Ages* (Oxford, 1952).

Souter, Alexander, *The Earliest Latin Commentaries on the Epistles of St. Paul* (Oxford, 1927).

Spicq, C., O.P., *L'Épître aux Hébreux* (Paris, 1952).

Stegmüller, Fridericus, *Repertorium Biblicum Medii Aevi.* 7 Vols. (Madrid, 1950-61).

Strauss, Gerhard, *Schriftgebrauch, Schriftauslegung und Schriftbeweis bei Augustin.* "Beiträge zur Geschichte der biblischen Hermeneutik," Vol. 1 (Tübingen, 1959).

Thimme, Hans, *Christi Bedeutung für Luthers Glauben. Unter Zugrundelegung des Romerbrief—des Hebräerbrief—des Galaterbriefkommentars von 1531 und der Disputationem* (Gütersloh, 1933).

Vogelsang, Erich, *Die Bedeutung der neuveröffentlichten Hebräerbrief-Vorlesung Luthers von 1517-18. Ein Beitrag zur Frage: Humanismus und Reformation* (Tübingen, 1930).

Zumkeller, Adolar, O.S.A., "Manuskripte von Werken der Autoren des Augustiner-Eremitenordens in mittel-europäischen Bibliotheken," *Augustiniana* 11 (1961) 27-86, 261-319, 478-532; 12 (1962) 27-92, 299-357; 13 (1963) 418-73; 14 (1964) 105-62.

INDEX OF NAMES

INDEX OF SUBJECTS